TEACHING DIVERSITY
THROUGH
CHILDREN'S LITERATURE

Kendall Hunt
publishing company

DR. KRISTEN BAZLEY
second edition
Kutztown University

M000309044

Cover and chapter opener images © Shutterstock, Inc.
Middle left cover image UnSplash/Annie Spratt. Middle cover image UnSplash/Capturing the human heart

Kendall Hunt
publishing company

www.kendallhunt.com
Send all inquiries to:
4050 Westmark Drive
Dubuque, IA 52004-1840

Copyright © 2015, 2019 by Kristen Bazley

PAK ISBN: 978-1-5249-8189-1
Text alone ISBN: 978-1-5249-8191-4

Kendall Hunt Publishing Company has the exclusive rights to reproduce this work,
to prepare derivative works from this work, to publicly distribute this work,
to publicly perform this work and to publicly display this work.

All rights reserved. No part of this publication may be reproduced,
stored in a retrieval system, or transmitted, in any form or by any means,
electronic, mechanical, photocopying, recording, or otherwise,
without the prior written permission of the copyright owner.

Published in the United States of America

Courtesy of Kristen Bazley

In loving memory of my Dad, Thomas D. Bazley III, PhD (1948–2018)

Table of Contents

Acknowledgements

I would like to express my gratitude to the many people, including friends and work colleagues, who saw me through this book venture; to include encouragement and suggested direction for this book; to those who read, wrote, and offered comments on the manuscript; and to those who gave invaluable assistance in the editing and proofreading process. I would be remiss not to single out the outstanding support I received from my publisher, Kendall Hunt and in particular my Project Coordinator, Noelle, for her guidance in bringing this book to publication, along with Tessa, my Acquisitions Editor, for offering this opportunity.

Specifically, I also wish to thank:

My parents for their unfailing encouragement, love, and support. Without them, I would not be where I am today.

Brian, for the never-ending support and encouragement shown to me throughout this and all ventures.

I wish to extend a special thanks to Ashlee Matelan, a graduate student at Kutztown University, for her help and contributions in making this second edition possible. Ashlee demonstrated a sincere interest in research and publication, and her hard work on this project is greatly appreciated.

CHAPTER 1

Introduction: Teaching Diversity and Multiculturalism through Children's Literature

Rawpixel/Shutterstock.com

The purpose of this book is to serve as a guide for classroom teachers in the elementary grades and for those who are preparing for this most rewarding of professions, to use children's literature in the teaching of diversity and multiculturalism. Traditionally, the role of children's literature in our elementary classrooms has been to develop reading skills and hopefully a love of reading. Children's literature also plays a role in other language arts skills including development of vocabulary, knowledge of grammar and punctuation, and writing skills. Without overemphasizing the obvious, children's literature is and has been a mainstay in our elementary grade curriculums, notwithstanding continual changes in how we teach, what we teach, and who we teach.

In fact, it is the changes in "who we teach" that provided the impetus behind this book. We are all familiar with the history of the origins and development of the United States of America. It is a country that was founded by immigrants and became and still is, a worldwide hub for immigrants who seek freedom from oppression and better economic opportunities for themselves and their families. The early immigrants were largely from Europe. However, coinciding with this early European immigration, this country also permitted the import of African immigrants against their will as slaves; a practice that ended only through a civil war that cost hundreds of thousands of American lives. Thus, while the "public face" of America in the 18th and 19th centuries mirrored that of Northern Europe, this country had a sizable African population, as well. However, for a hundred or more years after the slaves were freed, these now African Americans were not part of

Milles Studio/Shutterstock.com

mainstream society. They tended to live in segregated neighborhoods, were not well integrated into the U.S. workforce, and their children attended segregated schools. Thus, minority faces were seldom mingled among the predominantly white U.S. school population. The 1960s brought about major changes through legislation and court decisions that mandated the end of school segregation. Slowly, and painfully (for those opposed to school integration efforts), African American students became a far greater presence in traditionally and predominantly White U.S. public schools. Nevertheless, African American students continue to be a minority group in our classrooms and while hardly new arrivals to U.S. shores, they are among the racial and ethnic groups that are a focus of our efforts in teaching diversity and multiculturalism.

In the latter part of the 19th century and into the beginning of the 20th century, America continued to attract immigrants from Europe, although more so from Eastern and Southern Europe than in prior eras. Immigrants from China also arrived in the United States in the late 1800s and into the 1900s, often in response to labor needs and often smuggled into the country illegally.

The second half of the 20th century and into 21st century has seen an upsurge in Hispanic immigration into the United States. Most prominent in terms of numbers among these immigrants have been those from Mexico; although, many other Hispanic ethnicities/nationalities have also immigrated to the United States in sizable numbers. These include Puerto Ricans, who are U.S. citizens by virtue of their residence in a U.S. territory and thus, can freely relocate to any of the 50 states. However, ethnically Puerto Ricans fall under the Hispanic umbrella, to include Spanish being their primary, native language. Other Hispanic immigrants that have become prominent in the United

States are those from Cuba, Guatemala, Dominican Republic, Honduras, Nicaragua, and El Salvador. As these Hispanic groups have moved into the United States, a staggering increase in the number of Spanish-speaking students have made their presence in our public schools. In fact, U.S. Census findings

SSokolov/Shutterstock.com

show that over the past 30 years the bilingual population, including the Hispanic population, in the United States has increased from 23 million people to more than 60 million people—this translates to one in five Americans (Gandara, 2015).

Among other more recent immigrants to the United States are those from Eastern Europe, the non-Spanish–speaking Caribbean, India, and Southeast Asia. The point is that our heritage as a nation of immigrants is in fact, a living, and still evolving heritage. People from all over the world continue to seek residence in the United States and nowhere are the demographics of the world's peo-

ples more evident than in our public school classrooms. Hence the changes in "who we teach," which in turn has impacted what we teach and how we teach. The purpose of this book addresses the latter, that is, how can we teach diversity and multiculturalism through children's literature.

Markus Pfaff/Shutterstock.com

The What and the Why: Diversity and Multiculturalism

What do we mean by the terms, "diversity" and "multiculturalism" and why are they important in today's classrooms? We will address these questions in this section.

As outlined above, in any given classroom, we can have a microcosm of our current U.S. society, that is, White students whose roots in America have been well established for generations; to racial and ethnic minorities who are also long-time U.S. residents/citizens; to children who are relatively recent immigrants or whose parents are relatively recent immigrants. We can have children whose native/primary language is not English and/or with varying degrees of fluency in English. It is also quite possible that these children reside in neighborhoods that are *de facto* segregated; that is, they live among other people like themselves in terms of race and/or ethnicity, not because it is unlawful for them to live elsewhere but often because of limited economic means and/or personal choices such as ties to family, friends, and community. Yet, we bring these children all together into a classroom for the very important purpose of educating them, notwithstanding cultural differences and often language differences.

Can we be successful in providing an education to such a disparate group? The answer is clearly yes, but more than ever, we need to take special steps to familiarize students with each other in an effort to minimize differences and emphasize similarities. In doing so, we can diminish the notion of a "disparate group" and create a classroom environment where all students feel they "belong," where they can learn about their respective similarities and differences, and work with each other on learning activities. If we are to be successful in educating *all* students in our classrooms, we must create this type of inclusive, multicultural environment. Particularly for many minority and/or immigrant students, an inclusive classroom environment, along with a teacher who is sensitive to the special learning needs that many of these students may have, is paramount to their academic progress and success. As Echevarria, Frey, and Fisher (2015) have stated, culturally responsive teachers create an environment that values diversity and builds on students' different ways of learning, behaving, and using language.

Thus, addressing diversity and multiculturalism in our classroom curriculums (a) serves to broaden all students' cultural knowledge and fosters greater mutual respect and cooperation within our student bodies; (b) helps to provide a learning environment that will nurture the academic success of racial and ethnic minority students; (c) and hopefully, lays a foundation for cooperation and progress within the diverse society that is the United States of America.

What Is Children's Literature?

We won't belabor this subject here because Chapter 2 is devoted to exploring the full range of children's literature. You will find, however, that we do not offer an all-inclusive definition for children's literature. Rather, we describe it in terms of the various genres that make up this body

of literature. Nevertheless, for those who feel more comfortable with an all-inclusive definition, following is one put forth by Stoodt-Hill and Amspaugh-Corson (2009):

Elena Schweitzer/Shutterstock.com

> The term *literature* refers to a body of written works; it is an art form in which is used in creative, artistic ways. *Children's literature* is written specifically with children's interests and experiences in mind; this literature fosters children's passion for reading .... Most importantly, children's literature entertains children, while giving them access to the accumulated experience and wisdom of the ages. (p. 1)

Common Core and Teaching Diversity through Children's Literature

The *Common Core State Standards Initiative* defines "Common Core" as follows:

The Common Core is a set of high-quality academic standards in mathematics and English language arts/literacy (ELA). These learning goals outline what a student should know and be able to do at the end of each grade. The standards were created to ensure that all students graduate from high school with the skills and knowledge necessary to succeed in college, career, and life, regardless of where they live (Common Core State Standards Initiative, 2015a).

With regard to English language arts and literacy, the Common Core State Standards Initiative further describes these standards as certain critical types of content for all students, including classic myths and stories from around the world (Common Core State Standards Initiative, 2015b). To reiterate from above, this book provides a plan to merge children's literature with the teaching of diversity and multiculturalism. As will be outlined more fully in the following chapters, to do so involves introducing students to just this kind of children's literature, that is, classic myths and stories from around the world. Thus, the basic premise of this book fits squarely within the Common Core Initiative; a proposition that gains support from others who have recognized the value of children's literature when teaching subjects other than language arts (e.g., see McClure, Garthwait, & Kristo, 2015, p. 7).

How Can This Book Be Used and Why Will It Be Helpful?

This book is designed to provide guidance to teachers and prospective teachers in using children's literature to enhance and enrich their diversity and multicultural curriculums. It is also designed to be a resource for identifying appropriate children's literature that can be used in conjunction with diversity and multicultural curriculums as well as other supportive materials, both hard copy and in electronic format. Thus, this book is not intended to be a "one-time" read, but rather a volume that continues to be consulted by classroom teachers and students studying to become teachers, in their efforts to provide varied and effective learning activities associated with diversity and multiculturalism.

To be clear, teachers need in-depth coursework and/or in-service training to gain the necessary understanding of diversity and multiculturalism in order to successfully educate today's student population. This book may be used in conjunction with such courses/training but it is not a primary text on diversity and multiculturalism. Likewise, it is not a primary text covering children's literature. Ideally, current elementary teachers and prospective elementary teachers will have taken coursework on this subject. However, the premise being put forth here is that joining children's literature with other instructional efforts to inform and broaden awareness on diversity and multiculturalism will enhance student understanding and offer additional reading opportunities while doing so. This volume details a practical plan for achieving both of these outcomes. It is a "how to" book. The chapters that follow provide an overview of children's literature to ensure that all readers share a common understanding of this type of literature (Chapter 2); followed by a detailed discussion of how to bring children's literature into a diversity/multicultural curriculum (Chapter 3). Chapter 4 deals with the special circumstances that need to be considered for English Language Learners (ELL) when merging diversity/multiculturalism with children's literature. Chapter 5 explores opportunities to bring cultural experiences into classrooms by combining children's literature with both traditional and "high tech" pen pal activities.

Melpomene/Shutterstock.com

References

Common Core State Standards Initiative. (2015a). *About the standards.* Retrieved from http://www.corestandards.org/about-the-standards

Common Core State Standards Initiative. (2015b). *Key shifts in English language arts.* Retrieved from http://www.corestandards.org/other-resources/key-shifts-in-english-language-arts

Echevarria, J., Frey, N., & Fisher, D. (2015). What it takes for English learners to succeed. *Educational Leadership, 72*(6), 22–26.

Gandara, P. (2015). Rethinking bilingual instruction. *Educational Leadership, 72*(6), 60–64.

McClure, A. A., Garthwait, A., & Kristo, J. V. (2015). *Teaching children's literature in an era of standards.* Upper Saddle River, NJ: Pearson Education.

Stoodt-Hill, B. D., & Amspaugh-Corson, L. B (2009). *Children's literature: Discovery for a lifetime* (4th ed.). Boston, MA: Allyn & Bacon.

CHAPTER 2

An Overview of Children's Literature

Rawpixel/Shutterstock.com

This book is about using children's literature in the teaching of diversity and multiculturalism. But what is children's literature? Ideally, most of us have experienced and enjoyed reading children's literature in our early years, both as part of our formal education as well as informally at home, with family, in libraries, and so on. For those of us who teach or will soon become teachers, reading children's literature can still be a source of personal enjoyment as we use it to develop reading and language arts skills and knowledge in our students, as in expanded awareness/familiarization of cultures, ethnicities and races. However, do we remember specifically all the books we read as a child? Hopefully a few favorites can be recalled, but certainly many have been forgotten over time. Moreover, it is unlikely that in your younger reading years you were concerned about the various categories or genres of children's literature. Conversely, classroom teachers need to have an understanding and familiarization of these genres in order to expose students to the full array of children's literature. Such familiarization takes on special importance when using this literature for our purpose, that is, teaching diversity and multiculturalism.

This chapter answers the question posed at its outset: what is children's literature? The answer will not be provided in the form of a sweeping, all-inclusive definition. Rather, it will be addressed in a manner more useful to the classroom teacher who needs an understanding of the full scope of this type of literature in order to effectively incorporate it into the curriculum. It is answered by discussing the various genres of children's literature and providing examples and summaries of well-known works within each genre; together with works that would be particularly useful in teaching diversity and multiculturalism.

Children's Literature Genres
Contemporary Realistic Fiction

Fictional stories that are believable and cast in real-life settings; as opposed to fairy tales, folktales, and so on. These books allow the reader to see themselves or live through the characters' circumstances. Examples of contemporary realistic fiction books include: *Bud Not Buddy, Junie B Jones* series, and *Owl Moon*.

Recommended Contemporary Realistic Fiction for Teaching Diversity and Multiculturalism

One Green Apple by Eve Bunting

Summary: Farah, a Muslim immigrant and student in the United Stated notices some differences between her and her classmates. They all look different from people in her home country and they speak differently too. Throughout her field trip to an apple orchard, Farah starts to notice more and more similarities between her life before and her life now. Laughter sounds the same and she sees dogs that remind her of a dog she once had at home. Through this experience, Farah is confident that she will assimilate and feel more at home in time.

Fantasy

Fantasy is defined by the presence of magic and/or the supernatural. Fantasy stories often take place in an imaginary world and involve a journey or quest. The fantasy genre can include books labeled as High Fantasy, Low Fantasy, and Animal Fantasy. Popular fantasy stories include *Lord of the Rings* and *Alice and Wonderland.*

Recommended Animal Fantasy for Teaching Diversity and Multiculturalism

Chato's Kitchen by Gary Soto

Summary: Chato's Kitchen is written in "Spanglish," part English and part Spanish. Chato is a cat who thinks he has tricked a family of mice into "coming over for dinner" until the mice show up at his house with a canine friend. This is a funny, culture-laden book (e.g., food and dress) and highlights the fusion of the Spanish and English languages.

Historical Fiction

Historical fiction is made up of fictional stories that occur during a particular time or place in history. Examples of historical fiction books include: *Number of the Stars* by Lois Lowry, *Sarah Plain and Tall* by Patricia MacLachlan, and *Pink and Say* by Patricia Polacco.

Recommended Historical Fiction for Teaching Diversity and Multiculturalism

Me and Momma and Big John by Mara Rockliff

Summary: *Me and Momma and Big John* is a story set in the 1970s in New York City during a period of high unemployment. This book teaches children about the struggles in the 1970s of urban and impoverished living. Momma works hard to provide for John and his siblings as a stonecutter in the construction of a cathedral. Seeing how hard his mother works on such a small part of the construction causes John to realize how hard everyone around him is working. John wishes every person that cut stones for the cathedral would be noticed. John finds peace in knowing that the cathedral is a work of art, a work of art that his mother helped to create.

Nonfiction

Nonfiction books are factual accounts of people and events. Subgenres include autobiographies and biographies. An autobiography is a life history written by the subject of the book. Biographies are written about a particular person by another person who has studied the life of the subject. Examples of nonfiction books include: *Backyard Books: Are You A Dragonfly?* by Judy Allen, *An Egg Is Quiet* by Dianna Aston, and *Balloons Over Broadway: The True Story of the Puppeteer of Macy's Parade* by Melissa Sweet.

Recommended Nonfiction for Teaching Diversity and Multiculturalism

The Librarian of Basra: A True Story from Iraq by Jeanette Winter

Summary: This is a true story of a librarian from Basra, Iraq named Alia Muhammad. The library in Basra has always been a meeting place for community members to gather, read, and discuss books and community events. However, now with the war starting to reach Basra, Alia has to develop plans to protect, hide, and save the library's priceless book collection and watches, as the gunfire and bombs take over the city.

Poetry

A type of writing with a distinct style and rhythm that can include expression and figurative language.

Poetry Examples Include: *The Lorax* by Dr. Seuss, *The Giving Tree* by Shel Silverstein, and *The New Kid on the Block* by Jack Prelutsky.

Recommended Poetry for Teaching Diversity and Multiculturalism

Seasons of the Circle by Joseph Bruchac

Summary: *Seasons of the Circle* is a collection of poems. Each page represents a month of the year and includes a poem describing the life of Native Americans during that time. Readers can learn about Mountain Spirit Dancers, farming, and names of various Native American tribes.

Traditional Literature

Stories that are passed down by generations before us and change slowly over time. Subgenres of Traditional Literature include Legends, Tall Tales, Myths, Folk Tales, Fables, and Fairy Tales. Examples of traditional literature are *Stone Soup by Marcia Brown, The True Story of the 3 Little Pigs* by Jon Scieszka, *Ella Enchanted* by Gail Carson Levine and *The Tale of Peter Rabbit* by Beatrix Potter. This genre expands across cultures in that the same tales, like Cinderella, are told to fit the culture that is telling it.

Recommended Traditional Literature Story for Teaching Diversity and Multiculturalism

Lon Po Po: A Red-Riding Hood Story from China by Ed Young

Summary: One night, a mother left her three children at home while she went to visit her mother. Late that night, the children heard a knock on the door and heard the voice of someone claiming to be their grandmother, Po Po. The kids were skeptical about her voice, her furry feet, and her claws but the Po Po always had an excuse. It wasn't until the oldest child saw the wolf's face when she realized it was a wolf rather than their grandmother. The children end up outsmarting the wolf by teasing it from the top of the tree with gingko nuts where the wolf falls to his death.

This genre includes the following subgenres:

Legends, Tall Tales, and Myths

A legend is a story that is passed down by tradition and often believed to be true even though it is not proven to be. Legends differ from folktales because they are commonly viewed as an elaborated version of a historical event. Popular legends include: the classic tales of *Brer Rabbit* by Joel Chandler Harris and *The Legend of Sleepy Hollow* by Washington Irving.

Tall Tales are stories that have been exaggerated throughout time such as *Johnny Appleseed, Pecos Bill and Paul Bunyan.*

Myths are symbolic stories that explain the origins of the universe and relationships between gods and humans. Myths sometimes give a religious explanation and at times show how a particular custom began. Examples of myths include *Poseidon, God of the Sea, Prometheus*, and *Achilles and the Trojan War.*

Folktales

Because traditional stories are retold over and over again, folktales change with the passage of time. Folktales are often used to explain why things are the way they are. They may contain elements of fantasy but, overall, the stories seem logical. Folktales differ from legends because they are farther removed from historical accuracy. Examples of folktales include *Raven: A Trickster Tale from the Pacific Northwest* by Gerald McDermott.

Recommended Folktale for Teaching Diversity and Multiculturalism

The Talking Eggs: A Folktale from the American South by Robert D. San Souci

Summary: *The Talking Eggs* is an adapted Creole folktale about Blanche, a good-natured girl, and her greedy mother and sister. While fetching a pail of water, Blanche met a famished old woman and gave her some water. When Blanche returned home, she was scolded and smacked for returning with warm water. Scared to stay at home, Blanche wandered the forest until she met the old woman again. The old woman offered her a place to stay as long as she disregarded the magical, nonsensical happenings at the house. Blanche was respectful and did as she was told so, in turn, she was rewarded with luxuries her mother and sister had always dreamed of. After seeing the treasures, her mother encouraged her sister to go find the house and return with treasures like Blanche had. But, of course, the sister was not respectful and did not take the old woman seriously so she was punished. The mother and sister were chased by dangerous animals into the woods and Blanche lived happily ever after.

Fables

Fables are short stories used as moral lessons. Characters are often animals and inanimate objects that are given human qualities. Popular fables include: (a) *The Hare and the Tortoise,* (b) *The Country Mouse and the City Mouse,* and (c) *The Lion and the Mouse.*

Recommended Fable for Teaching Diversity and Multiculturalism

Fables by Arnold Lobel

Summary: This 1980 Caldecott Medal winner is a book that includes short fables that are no longer than a page in length. The lesson of each fable is clearly identified at the bottom of each fable.

Fairy Tales

In fairy tales, there is always a battle of good and evil and good always prevails. Fairy tales are full of magic and dreamlike components. Fairy tales are typically shorter than other works of fantasy. Popular fairy tales include *The Three Little Pigs* and *Rumplestiltskin.*

Recommended Fairy Tale for Teaching Diversity and Multiculturalism

Rapunzel retold by Rachel Isador

Summary: This story is told in an exotic African setting. Once upon a time, an evil sorceress watched as a man came into her garden and stole a plant named Rapunzel for his ailing wife. She confronted him one day and spared his life in exchange for his newborn child whom she named after the plant,

Rapunzel. She locked the child in a tower and kept her from the world, visiting her by climbing up her long locks of hair. Rapunzel caught the attention of a prince with her singing and he climbed up her hair to visit and they fell in love. Rapunzel was outcast when the sorceress discovered she was pregnant. Heartbroken and alone, the prince searched for Rapunzel for years in the wilderness until they were reunited and lived happily ever after with their children.

Picture Books and Chapter Books

Please note that these are not "genres", per say, but are important terms in children's literature you should know. Picture books tell a story with pictures or pictures and text. Chapter books, in comparison, usually have more text than pictures and tell the story through the text. Examples of picture books include: *Where the Wild Things Are* by Maurice Sendak, *The Very Hungry Caterpillar* by Eric Carle, and *Alexander and the Terrible, Horrible, No Good, Very Bad Day* by Judith Viorst. Examples of chapter books include: *Bud Not Buddy* and *Ramona the Pest*.

Recommended Picture Book for Teaching Diversity and Multiculturalism

Elmer by David McKee

Summary: Elmer the elephant has skin that looks like a rainbow quilt. He stands out from all the gray elephants. Not only is he colorful, Elmer makes all the other elephants laugh. On the inside, Elmer is bothered by his differences and paints himself gray in hopes he will fit in. As the rain washed his gray color away, the other elephants laughed at his disguise and Elmer realized that he did not mind standing out. He made the other elephants happy and, in return, that made him happy. Now once a year, in honor of Elmer's funny, unexpected disguise, the other elephants paint themselves bright colors and Elmer paints himself gray.

Presenting Children's Literature

While we will shift our focus more specifically on merging diversity and multiculturalism with children's literature in Chapter 3, let's not leave this overview discussion of children's literature, without considering some general teaching approaches for this important part of any elementary classroom curriculum. In this regard, the use of "read-alouds," that is, reading books to the class or groups of students, continues to be an important teaching strategy for introducing children's literature, especially for those from culturally diverse backgrounds. As Carbo (2008) suggests, this strategy affords students the opportunity to model accuracy, fluency, vocabulary and comprehension. Carbo also recommends that teachers provide books that are developmentally appropriate, if not out of the students' comfort zone, and are also of interest to them. It is important for teachers to encourage students to read for pleasure.

Courtesy of T.D. Bazley

Importance of Read-Alouds

Using read-alouds in the classroom should be a vital part of the daily curriculum. When choosing a read-aloud, the teacher should be aware of the following items:

- Introduce children to books and genres they might not otherwise read on their own. It provides them with a way to share books that many children are not yet ready to read on their own, but should be exposed to in order to ensure a rich literacy experience. It also allows teachers to bring rich vocabulary into the classroom and enthusiastically sell their love of reading.

- Reading aloud creates a classroom community by helping to build critical thinking skills.

- Discussions during and after read-alouds can be used to encourage students to create meaning in the text, connect ideas, connect to other texts, use their prior knowledge to understand the meaning, and comprehend the story.

- Reading aloud gives the students a chance to hear the teacher model fluency, tone, pitch, and expression.

- Read-alouds reach audio learners.

- Read-alouds with chapter books allow listeners to picture in their mind the story along with the setting, characters, and theme.

- Read-alouds help students develop good listening skills.

- Read-alouds help students compare and contrast stories by listening to a variety of books with similar stories.

- Read-alouds allow teachers to check for understanding by asking students questions to encourage and ensure comprehension.

The "Do's" and "Don'ts" of Read-Alouds

Do

1. Read aloud at least once a day.

2. Preview the book prior to reading it aloud.

3. Plan for questions and reactions on the book.

4. Introduce the book by showing the cover, illustrations, author, and title.

5. Read with EXPRESSION and don't be afraid to add in voices of the characters or sounds.

6. Give students a reason for listening (why will they like this book, what will they learn or what would you like them to get out of the read-aloud, etc.).

7. Read a wide variety of genres, styles, and texts.

8. Don't limit your read-aloud to only fiction.

9. Encourage making predictions and then, at the end, checking those predictions.

10. Reading nonfiction allows students to learn rich vocabulary and language.

11. Choose books with intriguing stories and interesting characters.

12. Check for comprehension, before, during, and after the read-aloud.

13. The teacher is not the only one who can do a read-aloud—students can read aloud to each other.

14. Watch your students for confusion or reactions while you are reading in order to gauge your technique.

15. HAVE FUN READING—you are your students model for reading. If you show your love of reading and sharing books, it will be contagious!

Don't

1. Read too fast or too slow.

2. Keep the book facing you—show those illustrations while you read (this is where knowing your book and practicing comes in handy).

3. Keep the pace or tone the same throughout the story.

4. Read aloud books you dislike yourself. This will show through during your read-aloud.

5. Keep reading a book that you realize was a bad choice (students are bored, uninterested, etc.). Watch the room and use that as your gauge. It is ok to express why you are changing books. However, model giving a book a chance and that some books just start off slow but get better (KNOW YOUR BOOK BEFORE READING IT!).

6. Don't overwhelm or read too long. It is ok to read the same book over a few days. Observe your audience and gauge based on age and ability to pay attention and listen.

7. Don't feel like you have to tie every read-aloud to something you are doing in class. You can just read a book aloud to model reading for enjoyment!

Examples of Books That Could Be Used as a Read-Aloud in the Classroom

Don't Push the Button by Bill Cotter

Summary: There is only one rule in the story *Don't Push the Button* and it is. . . Don't Push the Button!! Larry, the friendly monster in this book just can't take the temptation! When no one is looking, he convinces the reader to push it! What happens next in the story is sure to entertain the students and the teacher. This hilarious and interactive book is a great choice for a read-aloud and modeling expression, tone, pitch, voices, and even getting students to interact with the book.

Miss Nelson is Missing by James Marshall

Summary: Miss Nelson's class is the worst-behaved class in the whole school until Miss Nelson goes missing! Ms. Viola Swamp is their new, strict, substitute teacher. The kids were working so hard they became worried about Miss Nelson. They were searching and searching and could not find her anywhere. One morning, feeling extremely discouraged, they heard Miss Nelson's sweet voice! They were so excited to have her back that they forgot to misbehave. This silly story can help teachers begin a discussion for positive behavior management in the classroom. A great writing activity to tie into this read-aloud is to stop half way in the story and have students create Missing Posters for Miss Nelson. They can also make predictions on what happened to her or create their own written version of where they think she is. Once the stories or predictions are created, the teacher can finish the story and as a class students can compare and contrast their own endings with how the author ended the story. Finally, another lesson idea is having students practice their interviewing and public speaking skills by having them question teachers, faculty or other students about the whereabouts of Miss Nelson. (*Tip: Give your fellow teachers and faculty members a heads up that they may be questioned on where Miss Nelson is and ask them to have fun with it and be creative!)

Piggybook by Anthony Browne

Summary: Kids will laugh out loud as they read this book about Mrs. Piggot and her messy family. One day, she decides to leave for a little while. She left a note that said, "You are pigs" and they literally turn into pigs! Not only is this book fun to read aloud, but the pictures provide clues to the way the story unfolds. This book is a fun way to begin a discussion about responsibility and respect. Teachers can also have students make predictions at the beginning of the story and then tie in the importance of looking at the illustrations while reading or listening to a story. This book is a great example to demonstrate how clues shown in the illustrations but not stated in words can help them make or change their predictions as they read.

Somebody and the Three Blairs by Marilyn Tolhurst; illustrations by Simone Abel

Summary: *Somebody and the Three Blairs* is a reversed story of *Goldilocks and the Three Bears*. While the Blair family is at the park feeding the ducks, a little bear sneaks in and makes himself at home! When the Blairs return they are surprised to see that someone has been eating their food and playing with toys and sleeping in a bed! When read aloud with expression and excitement, this story can be fun and engaging for everyone. Students can also compare and contrast the various versions of the tale either independently or as a whole class activity. Another activity that could be used after this read-aloud, would be for students to create a sequencing chart/map.

The Little Mouse, The Red Ripe Strawberry, and THE BIG HUNGRY BEAR by Don and Audrey Wood; illustrated by Don Wood

Summary: This cute little story about a hungry little mouse who finds a strawberry in the woods. The only problem is that bears also love strawberries! The mouse takes the readers on quite an adventure as he tries to hide the strawberry from the bear! This book is perfect for showing the importance of inflection, expression, pace and enunciation while reading to children.

Questioning during Reading

While reading, ask a few open-ended questions such as:

kelvin tran/Shutterstock.com

- What do you predict will happen next?
- Has this ever happened to you?
- What is happening in the picture?

Connecting to Books

Have students make connections to the story. For example:

- **Text to Text**—Ask students if the book reminds them of something else they have read? Books you could use in the classroom that provide **Text to Text** connection opportunities are *Amazing Grace* by Mary Hoffman, *The Three Pigs* by David Wiesner and *The Three Little Wolves and the Big Bad Pig* by Eugene Trivizas.

- **Text to Self**—Do the events in the book remind students of something that has happened to them? Great **Text to Self** books for use in teaching this concept include *David Goes to School* by David Shannon, *I Need My Monster* by Amanda Noll and *Too Many Tamales* by Gary Soto.

- **Text to World**—Ask students how does this book relate to the world? *Number of the Stars* by Lois Lowry and *The Lorax* by Dr. Seuss are excellent choices to use when teaching students to look for **Text to World** examples. These are also wonderful books to discuss cultural aspects within the story.

Other instructional teaching strategies and aids that can be used when teaching diversity with children's literature include Venn Diagrams (for comparing two or more cultures as will be explained further in Chapter 3), KWL Charts (What the students already Know, What would they like to learn and What did they learn), Learning Logs, Shared Reading, Open-Minded Portraits, and Double-Entry Journals. This is not an inclusive list but a brief idea of what can be used. Teachers should also teach students how to choose books that are "just right" for them, books that are not too hard or too easy.

To learn more about these and other classroom strategies that you may want to use when teaching diversity through children's literature, view suggested websites and articles at the end of this chapter. The website referenced in the "Supplemental Resources for Teaching Diversity and Multiculturalism Through Children's Literature" section of this chapter, *Reading Rockets*, provides further details on these and other approaches that teachers might find effective in introducing children's literature to their students. In addition, teachers are always encouraged to develop their own unique approaches for developing high performing, enthusiastic readers in their classrooms.

Supplemental Resources for Teaching Diversity and Multiculturalism through Children's Literature
Articles

- Brashears, K. (2012). Appalachian picture books, read-alouds, and teacher-led discussion: Combating stereotypes associated with the Appalachian region. *Childhood Education, 88*, 30–34.

  Summary: For a region that encompasses so much of the United States, the Appalachian Region is often overlooked as far as cultural studies go. In fact, the Appalachian Region is full of culture and unique stories that would be great for the classroom. There needs to be a place for European-American literature despite the preconceived notions that European-Americans do not have a cultural identity or that it has been lost over the years. Brashears argues that there is a culture to be explored in Appalachia. This article provides readers with a list of picture books and summaries featuring the Appalachian Region.

- Gunn, A. (2014). Honoring my students' names! Using Web 2.0 tools to create culturally responsive literacy classrooms. *Childhood Education, 90*, 150–153.

  Summary: Gunn writes about cases where students have been renamed by their teachers simply because their teacher could not pronounce their name. This article makes a case for the importance of personal identity. Gunn provides readers a classroom lesson that encourages students to explore their own cultural identity while also building English vocabulary.

- Larson, J. (2013). *Talking with Jack Gantos*. Book Links.

  Summary: This interview with the author of *Rotten Ralph* and the *Joey Pigza* series, Jack Gantos, gives educators insight on what makes engaging children's books. The especially helpful piece of this article is the common core connection page. After reading this, educators will be able to teach Jack Gantos' books through comprehensive activities while aligning to the common core state standards.

- Louie, B. (2006). Guiding principles for teaching multicultural literature. *The Reading Teacher, 59*(5), 438–448.

  Summary: This article is a comprehensive guide for educators that reduces teaching multicultural literature down to its most essential elements. The stories should be authentic, the teacher should provide context for the culture being taught to promote a higher level of student understanding, as well as studying the main character(s) as an individual. Louie also includes a real-life classroom example about a unit she designed and facilitated based on different versions of the story, *Mulan*. She describes student reactions and activities that she used.

- Spicer, E. (2013). Common core state standards, nonfiction, and the need for common sense. *Library Media Connection*, 18–20.

  Summary: Spicer makes the argument that students, male and female, show interest in nonfiction texts at a young age. Read-alouds most often incorporate fictional texts but this research suggests that it is important for educators to model reading nonfiction texts as well. The Common Core has backed this idea of including more nonfiction texts in the classroom—the complexity of nonfiction texts help prepare students for the real world.

- Zunshine, L. (2014). What reading fiction has to do with doing well academically. *Style, 48*(1), 87–92.

  Summary: Zunshine argues that the Common Core goes against scientific cognitive research. The research she presents determines that fiction is generally superior to nonfiction when it comes to metacognitive complexity, which is what the Common Core wants in classroom reading materials. But the Common Core errs by pushing more informational texts and reducing fictional literature in the classroom.

Recommended Children's Literature Books

Aaron and Alexander by Don Brown

Summary: This is a story about the historical similarities of two American men, Alexander Hamilton and Aaron Burr. Both men were raised as orphans. Both men were heroic patriots of war and well-known public servants to our country. The pair were fierce rivals who took part in the country's most famous gun duel, only to learn that maybe there was room for them both after all.

A Dog Wearing Shoes by Sangmi Ko

Summary: One night a little girl named Mini and her parents found a dog wearing yellow shoes. The little girl wanted to keep the dog. Her mother agreed that the dog was lost but she didn't see the dog's family. They took him home where he began to bark. They took him for a walk in the park. Everyone loved him. While playing fetch, the dog in the yellow shoes ran away again! They searched for him everywhere and found him at a local shelter. Mini knew that a dog with yellow shoes had to have an owner who really missed him. She hung up signs to find the owner. The new owner was found right away and the next day Mini got a dog of her very own!

After the Fall by Dan Santat

Summary: This story takes place after Humpty Dumpty's widely known and humiliating fall. *After the Fall* is a story of perseverance as it describes how Humpty Dumpty bravely faced his fear of heights and learned how to fly.

Ally-saurus & the Very Bossy Monster by Richard Torrey

Summary: Ally-saurus loves to laugh and play with her friends. Then one day, a little girl named Maddie moves in and tries to be the boss. When Maddie starts making too many rules, Ally-saurus and her friends teach Maddie some new rules about being a good friend.

A Place to Start a Family by David L. Harrison; illustrated by Giles Laroche

Summary: This is a children's book of poems that describes both where and how animals live in their natural habitat. The educational poems and realistic illustrations in the book capture the reader's attention and hold it for the entire story.

A Time to Act: John F. Kennedy's Big Speech by Shana Corey and R. Gregory Christie

Summary: This nonfiction story invites the reader to get to know one of our country's greatest leaders. The life of John F. Kennedy aka "Jack" wasn't the same as people perceived it to be. He was the second of nine children. With the help of his family, he ran for Congress in 1946 and the rest is history. Jack became the youngest president in U.S. history on January 20, 1961. This book describes historical events that happened in the lives of the president and U.S. citizens as they struggled through the civil rights movements with the goal of creating "equal opportunity for all Americans." Even though President John F. Kennedy's life was cut short, his mission and promise of "equality" lives on for many Americans today.

Brave Girl by Michelle Markel (Biography)

Summary: This is an inspiring biography of a little girl named Clara who stages one of the largest strikes in U.S. history in an effort to bring more rights and better work conditions to women factory workers. This book encourages its reader to fight for what you believe in.

Give Bees a Chance by Bethany Barton

Summary: This informational book tells you everything you ever wanted to know about bees. The simple pictures and explanations help the reader to learn so many things about bees, including their anatomy, their jobs, and all of the ways bees make the world a better place.

The Gruffalo's Child by Julia Donaldson

Summary: *The Gruffalo's Child* has heard the scary stories of the Big Bad Mouse. One night he feels bored and a little bit brave and he leaves his cave in search of the Big Bad Mouse. As he walks through the forest in the middle of a snowstorm, he meets many animals with long tails and scary eyes, but nothing prepares him for what he sees next. The Gruffalo's Child shares the same sentiment of bravery as the original story *The Gruffalo* written by the same author.

Hidden Figures by Margot Lee Shetterly with Winifred Conkling; illustrated by Laura Freeman

Summary: *Hidden Figures* tells the story of four African American women who worked to defeat the odds set against them in the 1950s, when African American women were not accepted or respected in the workforce. Together, with determination and bravery, they worked behind the scenes to get the United States into space. This is a story of how their lives and the lives of all Americans changed forever.

I Am Afraid Your Teddy Is in Trouble Today by Jancee Dunn

Summary: This is a story about a teddy bear and his friends who are left home alone. They find themselves in a bit of trouble with the police after they were caught having a wild party. This story reminds its readers that police officers can be funny and like teddy bears too!

Jamie O'Rourke and the Big Potato by Tomie Depaola

Summary: This is an Irish Folktale about Jamie O'Rourke, the laziest man in Ireland and his story of tricking a leprechaun and a town full of people into helping him grow potatoes. This book teaches its readers that taking the easy way out is not always the best choice!

Courtesy of Kristen Bazley

Larry Gets Lost in Washington DC by John Skewes

Summary: Larry is a dog who travels to Washington, DC with his family. Larry becomes separated from his family and he begins to search everywhere for them. As he is searching for his boy, he learns a lot about our nation's capital and even meets a new friend along the way!

One Proud Penny by Randy Siegel and Serge Bloch

Summary: This informational/nonfiction book takes the reader on an adventure through the life of a penny. Born in Philadelphia, this penny knows all about the Liberty Bell, the Philly cheesesteaks, and more. This is a story that helps its readers understand how the penny is small and there are millions of them but together they stand proud and can change the world.

Penguins Don't Wear Sweaters by Marikka Tamura; Illustrations by Daniel Rieley

Summary: This is a story about a family of penguins happily living a normal life when something begins floating in the water near their home. An oil spill puts the penguins in danger. Suddenly people are coming and trying to help. People are making them sweaters but penguins don't wear sweaters! This story shows the effects of helping others out of a sticky situation.

The Geese March in Step written and illustrated by Jean Francois Dumont (Picture Book)

Summary: This is a story of imagination and individuality as the reader learns of a small gosling named Zita and her struggle to fit in with the rest of her flock. The leader of the flock named, Igor, is frustrated by Zita when she can't march in time with the other geese. He kicks her out of the parade and the geese continue on. Back at the farm, Zita decides to have her own parade with her other farm animal friends and soon becomes the new leader of her very own parade.

The Mermaid by Jan Brett

Summary: *The Mermaid* by Jan Brett is an under-the-sea version of Goldilocks and the Three Bears. Kiniro, a young mermaid, swims upon a gorgeous house made of seashells and coral. She is so curious that she goes inside. She's so excited to find a just-right breakfast, pretty little chair, and, even, a comfy bed that rocks in the current. When the octopus family returns to their house, they immediately sense that something fishy has been going on!

The Secret Subway by Shana Corey

Summary: This is a historically accurate story with captivating illustrations about the transformation of New York City. Beginning in the 1860s, the story describes what the dirty city looked like and the chaos of how people got around. At the time, everyone had ideas of change but no one knew what to do. Alfred Ely Beach is described in the story as a THINKER and a man of ACTION and this is his story of the long-forgotten creation of New York City's underground train.

The Skydiving Beavers: A True Tale by Susan Wood; Illustrated by Gysbert van Frakenhuyzen (Nonfiction, Biography, Diversity)

Summary: This is a nonfiction story that is almost too crazy to be true! In the 1940s the growing town of McCall, Idaho became a popular destination to live due to its beautiful mountains, sparkling lakes, fresh mountain air. . . and too many beavers! The people had a problem and so did the beavers. The solution? Move the beavers! But how? Parachutes! This is a true story of how one man named Elmo and one beaver named Geronimo moved a bunch of beavers to their new home.

The Youngest Marcher by Cynthia Levinson (Nonfiction)

Summary: Audrey Faye Hendricks was a 9-year-old girl who wanted to be just like everybody else. The problem was that segregation laws did not allow that. Influenced by a family friend, Mike aka Dr. King, Audrey became determined to break down the barriers that limited her life. She was even willing to go to jail! This is a true story about an inspiring and determined little girl who bravely played a big role in the civil rights movement.

When I Was Young in the Mountains by Cynthia Rylant; illustrated by Diane Goode

Summary: This is a story based on the early life of Cynthia Rylant. The modest story and humble illustrations detail the simplistic lifestyle of a happy little girl who was visiting her grandparents in a little town in the Appalachian Mountains of Virginia.

Useful Websites for Your Classroom

- **100 Great Children's Books:** http://www.nypl.org/childrens100

  The New York Public Library has compiled 100 must-read books for children. These books have stood the test of time and will entertain diverse learners. Reader reviews can help influence which books educators would want to read with their students.

- **Carol Hurst's Children's Literature Site:** http://carolhurst.com/

  Carol Hurst doesn't just list books. She writes a review, identifies discussion points, provides several activities, and even points out related books for each and every children's book on her website. Books are listed by theme, genre, and curricular subject. You will definitely find what you're looking for!

- **Multicultural Children's Literature:** http://www.multiculturalchildrenslit.com/

  Organized by culture, ranging from African to Jewish, this website lists children's books to help teach children about people from other cultural backgrounds. Each book selection contains a summary to help teachers easily select materials for their class.

- **Multicultural Literature:** http://ccbc.education.wisc.edu/books/multicultural.asp

  Not only does the website define multicultural literature, the book lists are broken down by culture and by the grade level of the text. These book lists contain popular works as well as some lesser-known stories.

- **Reading Rockets: Classroom Strategies:** http://www.readingrockets.org/strategies

  Teachers may explore a variety of teaching strategies and aids for presenting children's literature to their students.

- **Role of Multicultural Literature**: http://www.eduplace.com/rdg/res/literacy/multi1.html

    This website provides a brief, yet informative argument about the role of multicultural literature in the classroom.

Good Literature Definitions to Know

Antagonists

An antagonist character or characters are one(s) who are in conflict with the main character, also known as the protagonist.

Characters

The people/animals/creatures, and so on in the story.

Graphic Novels

Graphic novels are stories that are told in a comic book style. Graphic novels address many topics and can be fiction or nonfiction.

Graphic Organizer

Graphic organizers are a great way to organize thoughts, parts of a story, and information. They can help students identify the important parts of a story or help distinguish fact/fiction or nonfiction/fiction items as they read.

KWL Charts

KWL charts help students figure out what they know prior to reading a book or learning about a topic (activating prior knowledge), what the students want to learn by reading the book or researching the topic and then at the end, what they learned after reading the book or completing their research on the topic. This can be done independently or as a whole class shared activity.

Literary Criticism

Literary criticism is the study, an interpretation or assessment of a piece of literature.

Literary/Story Elements

This includes the character(s), setting(s), theme(s), problem(s), and solution(s).

Motif

Motif is a recurrent idea in a piece of literature that can develop or explain the theme.

Protagonist

The protagonist is usually the main character of the story/book. Readers usually identify him or her as the "good guy."

Reader Response

Reader responses are what readers bring to the story prior to reading a text, what happens during reading and how they feel about what they have read.

Readers Theater

When students perform part of a story. They can read the story right from the book, paper, or script. This may but does not have to include dressing or using props. Through Readers Theater students are able to practice public speaking, expression, tone, and pitch.

Setting

Where a story takes place. A story can have more than one setting within the same book.

Story's Central Idea

The main element of the story that is the most important central part of it.

Theme

The definition of theme in a story is the overall meaning, point or "main idea."

Commonly Asked Literature-Based Questions

What is a DRTA?

Directed Reading Thinking Activity. This is a comprehension strategy that helps a student to think of important questions to ask about a text and either confirm or fix their predictions. It also helps readers activate prior knowledge and become better at monitoring their own understanding of what they are reading. Good book for DRTA is *Cloudy with a Chance of Meatballs* by Judi and Ron Barrett.

What is the five-finger rule to choose the right book?

This is a tip for helping a student choose the right book for them to read independently.

1. Choose a book

2. Open the book to any page

3. Put one finger up for each word you don't know.

    0–1 Book is too easy

    1–2 Book is perfect for me

    3–4 Book might be too hard for me

    5 Book is too hard for me

What are a few of the awards for literature and illustrations of children's books?

- **Newbery Medal:** medal that is awarded annually by the American Library Association to an outstanding children's book.

- **Caldecott Medal:** an award presented each year by the American Library Association to the author of an outstanding picture books.

- **Robert F. Sibert Informational Book Award:** given annually to the author of the most distinguished informational book from the preceding year.

- **The Coretta Scott King Award:** an award is given out to distinguished African American authors and illustrators of books for children and young adults.

What is prereading and what are some examples?

Activities that can be done before reading. Some examples of these would be KWL charts, anticipation guides, and contrast charts.

What is postreading and some examples of it?

Activities that can be done after reading. Some examples of these are Venn diagrams, book trailers, and book charts.

What are during reading activities and some examples of them?

Activities done during reading. Some examples are literature circles, journals, and graphic organizers.

What is the author's purpose?

The author's purpose is for what reason they wrote a book. A way to figure this out is for the reader to ask themselves if the book made them happy, sad, angry, or excited. If it did then the purpose was to entertain, while a book that is very opinionated and trying to get the reader to agree with the author is for the purpose of persuasion. Lastly, there are books that are to inform, or are full of facts.

What are the Molly Bang Principles?

These are different principles about what our eyes are drawn to when looking at pictures. They have to do with shapes, colors, placement, and light.

How do you determine what book is appropriate for a child?

For books to be appropriate for a child, they should be in their appropriate reading level.

Courtesy of T.D. Bazley

Books should be appropriate as independent readers, books that are at reading level that the teacher can help guide through or appropriate interest level, that someone else can read but the book is the student's age and grade.

What is the difference between interest level and reading/grade level?

Interest level is the grade range at which the children would be interested in a certain book, such as two to five would be second to fifth graders. Reading/grade level is the grade level at which the reader should be able to read the book without difficulty.

Why/how does creating a song or script help teachers assess what students know about the elements of literature?

Students have to be able to understand information such as the literary elements in order to utilize that information in writing a song or script. This is an assessment that allows students to be creative as well as use the knowledge they have gained, rather than just write it down in a book. They can also be assessed on the ability to use some sort of expression, tone, and pitch as well as detail to relay the story to the teacher and the class.

What are some examples of illustration techniques? Why is it important to teach about illustration techniques?

Some artists use different mediums for their illustration, whether they be paints (the type could differ), charcoals, photographs, and so on. It is important for children to know and recognize this when they are looking at the artwork in stories. They should be paying attention to the details and what catches their eye!

Why is it important to read stories with real-life challenges?

Reading books with real-life challenges is important so students who are struggling won't feel so alone if they have a character to connect with that is dealing with similar vices. It also teaches empathy and compassion for all students to learn about differences.

What are text sets and how can they be used in the classroom? Why should they be used? What is the purpose of a text set?

Text sets are groups of books by genre, author, subject, illustrator, or some other pertinent information. These should be used to get students interested in the various types of books that are available or at least give them options. Text sets should also have a visual component surrounding the books to attract the attention of the students. For example, a text set on the ocean could be placed on blue bulletin board paper cut out in wave shapes, fish cutouts, and stuffed animal whales and sharks. Text sets can be randomly selected and displayed on a specific topic or they can tie in with a specific part of the curriculum that the students are currently learning about.

How do you select books for the classroom?

You need to take into account the authors and illustrators, the illustrations and text, the reading levels, interest levels, subject matter, and the many genres. Also, considering the different awards that some books have. Teachers must select books based on student interests but also books that will challenge them and introduce them to new genres and topics.

What are inferences? What would be a good book to teach inferences?

Inferences are guesses about what is going on in a story. There are clues in pictures or text that help with inferences. Two books to teach about inferences are *Tuesday* by David Weisner and *Elmer* by David McKee.

What are predictions? What would be a good book to teach about making predictions?

Predictions are guesses about what is going to happen in a story. Illustrations and words in a book can help to get the students ready to predict. Two books for this would be *Measuring Penny* by Loreen Leedy or *Somebody and the Three Blairs* by Marilyn and Simone Abel.

What is personification? What would be a good book to teach about personification?

Personification is giving life like qualities to something that isn't alive. A book to teach about this would be *The Runaway Dinner* by Allan Ahlberg.

What is descriptive writing? What is a good book that would demonstrate this type of writing?

These are important things that show how someone feels, what they do or paints a picture about something that has happened. Two books for this would be *Charlotte's Web* by E. B. White or *Owl Moon* by Jane Yolen.

What is persuasive writing? What is a good book that would demonstrate this type of writing?

Persuasive writing is writing to persuade with your opinion in the hope that the reader will agree with you. Good examples of this would be *The True Story of the Three Little Pigs* by Jon Scieszka and *Don't Let the Pigeon Drive the Bus* by Mo Willems.

What would be good books to teach story sequencing with?

The True Story of the Three Little Pigs by Jon Scieszka and *Too Many Tamales* by Gary Soto.

What is visual imagery?

When a reader creates an image of the story in their mind. Students use their background and prior knowledge to help them create these images before, during, or after reading. This is also a good strategy to have English language learner (ELL) students explain the images they see when reading a book from their culture and how background and experiences impact how different people with different backgrounds can view the same book differently.

What are good books to teach visual imagery with?

Aesop's Fables by Jerry Pinkney or *Tales of a Fourth Grade Nothing* by Judy Blume.

Reference

Carbo, M. (2008). Strategies for increasing achievement in reading. In R.W. Cole (Ed.). *Educating everybody's children: Diverse teaching strategies for diverse learners* (2nd ed.) (pp. 98–122). Arlington, VA: Association for Supervision and Curriculum Development.

CHAPTER 3

Teaching Diversity through Children's Literature: The Why and the How

Rawpixel/Shutterstock.com

In Chapter 1, we addressed the major premises of this book: (a) we live in an increasingly cultur-ally diverse society and nowhere is this diversity more manifest than in our school classrooms; (b) research that suggests our educational efforts will be enhanced if we teach our students about the diverse cultures that populate our classrooms; and (c) children's literature can assist in this process. Chapter 2 defined and provided an overview of children's literature in order to establish a common understanding of this type of literature and general teaching strategies associated with this subject. Now in Chapter 3, we address the "Why" and the "How" of using children's literature as a tool in teaching diversity.

Let's review what we know about classroom diversity. Students must realize that all people do not share the same cultural norms or language. Even cultures can vary within different groups speaking the same language (Kovarik, 2014). Moreover, not all students are even aware of their own attitudes (Cruz, Ellerbrock, Vasquez, & Howes, 2014). In summarizing the impact of culture in the classroom Dack and Tomlinson (2015) stated:

> All people are shaped by the culture in which they live. The shaping process is both subtle and pervasive, and it can be difficult for all of us to grasp that people shaped by other cultures will see and respond to the world differently than we do. After all, our own cultural lenses seem so "natural"—so "right". The consequences of this cultural blindness can range from comedy to awkwardness to waste of human potential (p. 11).

Our goal through this book and in partic-ular this chapter, is to address this cultural blindness by enhancing cultural aware-ness and thus any avoiding moments of comedy and awkwardness at the expense of and embarrassment to, a student who is misunderstood by other classmates; and

Rawpixel/Shutterstock.com

to generally create a classroom environment that will foster all students to reach their full potentials. This type of environment will help students feel at home in their classroom which in turn, will lead to greater academic success.

Why teach Diversity through the use of Children's Literature? As a veteran teacher, I have found that incorporating children's literature into my classroom is a key to teaching students about diversity. Am I alone, or a pioneer in this regard? Hardly! For example, Anderson (2009) stated that good multicultural literature increases readers' appreciation of different cultures and helps them overcome any stereotypical views they may have.

Likewise, Dack and Tomlinson (2015) recognized that literature, along with music are effective tools for teaching children about different cultures. No doubt, other forms of media and the arts to include theatre, cinema, television, and the visual

Courtesy of T.D. Bazley

Courtesy of T.D. Bazley

arts all have value in broadening the cultural horizons of students. One popular example of theatre and cinema (that combine music and dance, as well), that is both appealing to children as well as providing a cultural experience is *The Lion King*. Even some theme parks such as Disney's *Animal Kingdom* and *Epcot*, can offer children both an enjoyable and educational adventure into different cultures.

Although some students may have the good fortune of going on a field trip to a movie, cultural museum, theatrical performance, or even a theme park, on a more routine/daily basis incorporating into the classroom diversity curriculum children's literature that reflects and introduces a variety of cultures to students will broaden their cultural horizons; along with providing all-important reading opportunities.

Courtesy of T.D. Bazley

Children can relate to characters in a book and literature can help to foster understanding and empathy with people who are different from themselves in order to transcend the differences. Development of a concept of self-identity is facilitated in minority students who read children's literature that reflects their own backgrounds (Irizarry, 2015). Along these lines, Echevarria, Frey, and Fisher (2015) have stated that making connections between historical events and how they might have affected a student's native culture is an effective way to connect content to diverse learners; thus making the case for children's literature that recounts historical events outside of the United States. Clearly, incorporating diverse children's literature into the elementary classroom has much to offer in terms of enhancing students' multicultural awareness.

How to Incorporate Children's Literature into Diversity Education

This need not be a daunting task or undertaking. We first consider some important "do's" to lay a sound foundation for diversity education through children's literature. We then examine a key teaching step in this process, followed by specific classroom activities that can be used to incorporate children's literature into teaching students about other cultures.

The "Do's"

1. Have a variety of diversity/culture-based books in your classroom library. In Chapter 2, we explored the wide range of genres that fall under the banner of children's literature. In stocking your classroom library, be conscious of not only selecting a broad array of genres, but also ensure that in each genre there are books that reflect a wide range of cultures in terms of authors and story lines.

2. It is especially important to include in your classroom library children's literature that reflects the cultures, races, and ethnicities of your students.

3. Take time to discuss cultural aspects of the literature you read to your class, or they read independently. In order to understand the story, cultural aspects may need to be explained prior to reading it.

4. As a classroom teacher, you should emphasize similarities or differences of people from various ethnic or cultural backgrounds while introducing different types of literature. The needs, emotions, and concerns that all humans share, need to be highlighted as similarities that unite us.

5. Encourage students to research websites about the authors they are reading as well as the geographic and cultural settings that are portrayed in their books. Johnson (2015) touted that using technology is one

Courtesy of T.D. Bazley

Courtesy of T.D. Bazley

of the last means of adapting materials for diversity and gathering information about many cultures.

6. Have high expectations for all students (Cole, 2008). Moreover, view all students as individuals in order to attend to their varied points of readiness, their interests, their exceptionalities, their status among peers, and so on, when planning curriculum and instruction (Dack & Tomlinson, 2015).

7. It is imperative to put all your thoughts and prejudices aside about a culture as students will pick up on that. Never degrade a culture or make negative comments regarding a specific culture. Teachers should value each student's view of the world. The student's view is colored by the culture in which they are immersed (Dack & Tomlinson, 2015). Classrooms should be a safe place for students to explore diversity: their own culture, the culture of others, and all the preconceived notions (Cruz et al., 2014).

8. Teachers must learn all the students' names and be able to pronounce them correctly. (Gonzalez-Mena, 2014).

9. Teachers should expect that not all families speak English (Gonzalez-Mena, 2014).

Culture as Portrayed in Children's Literature

How is culture portrayed in children's literature, so that it can be used to expand students' cultural awareness? Common attributes of culture include language, religion, holidays, family structure, food, dress, housing, and occupations (with the latter four impacted by geographic region and climate). In summary

Courtesy of T.D. Bazley

Table 3.1 Summary of Cultural Characteristics Commonly Portrayed in Children's Literature (Example of What Teachers Could Fill Out with Students)

Culture	Language(s) spoken	Primary religion	Major holidays celebrated	Unique to that culture	Food unique to that culture
Indian	Hindi	Hinduism	Holi and Diwali	Hatha Yoga "Namaste": a greeting; Temples	Mango: national fruit Lotus: national flower
Chinese	Chinese	Buddhism	Chinese New Year Lantern festival	Every year is represented by an animal; Grooms pays the bridesmaids for the right to take the bride; Lion dance Great Wall	Rice Shark Fin Soup; Szechuan seasoning; Tea
Jewish	Hebrew	Judaism	Hanukkah Yom Kippur Passover	Synagogue/ temple; Rabbi The torah Menorah Dreidel	Latkes Challah Matzah Balls
African-American	English	Christian Denominations	Christmas Kwanza	Many are descendants of slaves; Blues/Jazz/ Hip-Hop; Civil rights movement	Collard Greens Cornbread Biscuits Chitterlings Okra
Latino/ Hispanic	Spanish	Roman Catholic	Christmas Independence Day; from colonial rulers	Traditional Brightly colored clothing; Escondidas ("Hide and Seek"); Pinata	Flan Tamales Moles Tortillas Porc Chuc Ceviche
Arab	Arabic	Islam	Ramadan	Oil is the most abundant natural resource; Desert environment; A primary working animal is the camel	Hummus Falafel Tahini Tabouleh Pita Bread Tea

fashion, Table 3.1 identifies cultural characteristics of selected racial and ethnic groups that are commonly portrayed in children's literature. Identifying these attributes to your students as they read diverse children's literature is a key to advancing their cultural knowledge.

Using Children's Literature in Teaching Diversity—Classroom Activities

There are any number of classroom activities that can be used to teach diversity. While I will outline some of them in the following paragraphs, I also encourage teachers to use their own creative "genius" to develop other effective strategies. Referring again to Table 3.1, the format of this table can be used as a learning activity wherein students can investigate different cultures and then complete their own table listing holidays, religion, language, traditions, and food for the subject of their research.

Courtesy of T.D. Bazley

Another activity I used in the classroom was teaching culture through a variety of nonfiction children's literature books that represented different countries. We would read different books and examine the cultural aspects of that country. I have provided an example of a template (see Figure 3.1) students would complete as we worked our way around the world reading these books. Depending on grade level, these charts could be filled out together as a whole class or individually as we read these books together and then discuss the different cultural aspects. Then we would examine the differences to our own cultures including our classroom culture. Students then would complete a Venn diagram (See Figure 3.2) that allowed the students to read a book on a culture that is of interest to them and then compare that culture to their own. They would then find similarities and indicate those on the Venn diagram. There are many ways that culture can be appreciated across disciplines. For example, every culture can point to its own great thinkers and others who have made major contributions to humankind.

Figure 3.1 Directions: After reading a children's non-fiction book(s) on a different culture, fill out the chart to help you examine the similarities/differences to your own culture.

	Title/Author
	Culture
	Dress
	Language/New Vocab
	Food
	Similarities to your culture
	Differences from your culture

Culture 2

Culture 1

Courtesy of Ambria Liles

Figure 3.2 Directions: Use this Venn Diagram Chart to compare the different cultures as you read books to the class. This activity can be done either with the class as a whole, in cooperative groups or individually.

Students would then use a template of a world map that was given to them to mark what country the story came from. Alternatively, set up a world map and each time they learn about a new place via literature they put a star on the map. This is a great way to join social studies and geography with cultural awareness, using children's literature. Another activity along these lines is to ask students to bring in postcards received from family members or friends from places to which they have traveled to or perhaps reside in. Then based on the location portrayed on the postcards, have the children find books and information, and so forth on these places. Using these types of activities will provide students visual evidence of the many cultures they have explored over the course of the school year.

Courtesy of T.D. Bazley

Courtesy of T.D. Bazley

Serban Bogdan/Shutterstock.com

I also explored holidays around the world when teaching about different cultures and diversity. Groups of students would be paired with a particular culture and we would read children's books from that culture, as a class.

Students would be encouraged to select their own culture or a culture they had interest in learning more about. They would then learn the holiday traditions and we set up booths around the room. Then students would dress in the native clothing, have information at their booth about the holidays of that culture, several books on the culture, and prepare a food item that is eaten during a holiday specific to the culture. Then for a designated period of time students would rotate around the room hearing the presentations of their fellow classmates on the culture and holidays. In order to simulate their world travels, students would make their own passports and obtain entry stamps at each country's booth.

Perhaps a more advanced activity first involves the class reading the traditional version of *Cinderella* followed by one or more cultural variations of this same story and compare the different versions using a Venn Diagram (See Figure 3.3). Then have students research their own or another culture for the purpose of writing their own, unique culturally oriented version of *Cinderella* based on what they learned. This can be done as a class in the primary grades where students orally contribute narrative and create their own character illustrations. Whereas intermediate level students have more advanced writing skills, they can work independently on creating their *Cinderella* cultural versions. Students could use a template to assist them in their writing depending on grade level. Examples of such a templates are found at Figures 3.4 and 3.5. Students can then create an image of the Cinderella portrayed in their story using

Zlatko Guzmic/Shutterstock.com

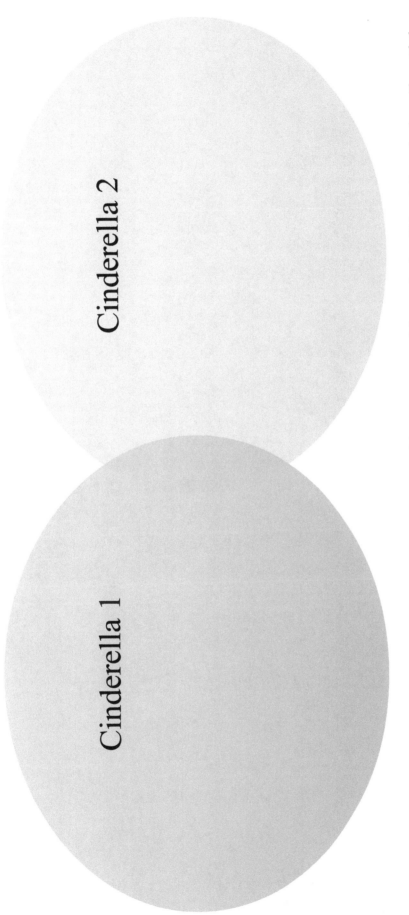

Figure 3.3 Directions: Use this Venn Diagram Chart to compare the different versions of the story as you read them to the class. This activity can be done either with the class as a whole, in cooperative groups or individually.

Courtesy of Ambria Liles

Figure 3.4: Cinderella around the World

Directions: After examining several cultural Cinderella stories, complete the following to help you write your own version based on elements specific to your life and culture.

My story is based on the following culture: _____

Cinderella's name in this culture: _____

She has _____ siblings.

She wears:

_____

_____

_____

_____

She meets _____.

She loses her: _____

Additional info as it relates to her culture:

_____

_____

_____

Figure 3.5: Cinderella and Culture Comparison Chart

Directions: Use this chart to compare different versions of Cinderella we are reading in class and the cultures they represent.

	Title/Author
	Setting
	Plot
	Characters
	Problem/Resolution
	Cultural Uniqueness (how is this culture different from mine and/or other ones I have read about)
	New Vocab from this culture, that I did not know and the definitions
	Culture I would like to examine next and the book I would like to read

construction paper or other materials. This image should reflect dress that is consistent with the cultural orientation of the story.

The following are examples of cultural variations of *Cinderella* that can be used in connection with this activity.

"Cinderella" Books

Adelita: A Mexican Cinderella Story written and illustrated by Tomie DePaola

Summary: The Mercados were thrilled to be having their first child. They called Esperanza, a woman close to the family since she was a girl, to come care for the mother and new child. Sadly, the mother passed away shortly after Adelita's birth. However, Adelita lived happily with her father and Esperanza and grew up to be a beautiful, kind woman. Adelita's father eventually remarried and Esperanza had a funny feeling about the stepmother and stepsisters from the very beginning. After Adelita's father died unexpectedly, the stepmother was very cruel to Adelita and had Adelita do all of Esperanza's house duties and sent Esperanza away. Similar to other Cinderella stories but with a more realistic plot, the family is invited to a party where an eligible bachelor, Javier, would be looking for a wife. Esperanza returns to the house to make sure Adelita goes to the party in her mother's hidden treasures. Adelita wins Javier's heart and they live a happy life together.

Unique words/phrases from this cultural Cinderella story for class discussion:

- **Me hace muy feliz saberlo**—I am so happy

- **La Casa Mercado se Lleno de Algeria**—the Mercado house was full of happiness

- **Que Frias Son**—they're cold ones

- **Entre Lagrimas y Abrazos**—amid tears and hugs

- **Maldad y Vinagre**—meanness and vinegar

- **Mis Hijas**—my daughters

- **Una Fiesta en su Hacienda**—a party at their ranch

- **Y Punto**—that is final

- **Mi Pequeñita**—my little one

- **Un Sueño**—a dream

- **Cuarto de Tiliches**—storeroom

- **Rebozo**—shall

- **Vamonos**—let's hurry

- **Cencienta**—Cinderella

- **Gracias**—thank you

- **Zapatilla de cristal**—glass slipper

- **Principe**—prince

Cendrillon: A Caribbean Cinderella written by Robert D. San Souci and illustrated by Brian Pinkney

Summary: Written from the Godmother's point of view, this Caribbean version is similar to the traditional Cinderella tale. Cendrillon works her hands to the bone until her godmother, who has been given a magic wand, uses all her magic to give Cendrillon the night of her life at the ball. Cendrillon falls in love with Paul and he goes in search of her with her missing slipper. They were married and lived happily ever after.

Unique words/phrases from this cultural Cinderella story for class discussion:

- **Bonjour**—hello

- **Bebe**—baby

- **Blanchisseuse**—a wash woman

- **Fet**—a party

- **Fruit a pain**—breadfruit

- **Gwo-ka**—lively dance and big drum

- **Manicou**—an opossum

- **Tremblant**—a pin

- **Nannin**—godmother

- **Monsieur**—Sir

Fair Brown and Trembling: An Irish Cinderella Story written and illustrated by Jude Daly

Summary: Trembling's beauty made her sisters very jealous so they left her at home to do the cooking while they went to church. A magic henwife told Trembling that she should be in church and quickly crafted her a beautiful gown and shoes to wear. In the meantime, the henwife cooked the meal so that when Trembling returned, it was as if she never left. Trembling did this three times and each time she would rush back home so that her sisters would not know. The third time she left behind a slipper so the Prince finally had something to help him search for her. Trembling married the Prince and they had many, many children.

Unique words/phrases from this cultural Cinderella story for class discussion:

- **Henwife**—a woman who raises poultry

- **Lily**—flower

- **Beggar**—someone who begs for food or money

David Carillet/Shutterstock.com

Mufaro's Beautiful Daughters: An African Tale written and
illustrated by John Steptoe

Summary: Mufaro had two beautiful daughters but on the inside, the daughters were very different. One daughter, Manyara, was hateful and conniving—the other, Nyasha, was kind and full of empathy. It was Nyasha who fed the hungry and was kind to the undesirable so she becomes queen much to the dismay of Manyara who becomes her sister's servant.

Unique words/phrases from this cultural Cinderella story for class discussion:

- **Millet**—group of small-seeded grasses and very important crops in Asia and Africa

- **Yams**—the stem of a tropical plant *Dioscorea batatas* and usually sweeter than a sweet potato

- **Silhouetted**—is the image of something that is represented as a solid shape in usually the color black and has its edges matching the outline of the image

- **Weavers**—person who makes cloths

zcw/Shutterstock.com

Smoky Mountain Rose: An Appalachian Cinderella written by Alan Schroeder and illustrated by Brad Sneed

Summary: Smoky Mountain Rose is about a southern family in the Smoky Mountains. The heavy dialect makes it a fun read aloud for students of all ages! Rose was living a hard life under the thumb of her stepmother, when their rich neighbor, Seb, invited all the locals to a party. Thanks to a normal-looking, yet magical pig, Rose was able to go to the party in style. Keeping to the tradition of returning the glass slipper, Rose and the "rich feller," Seb grow old together in the mountains.

Unique words/phrases from this cultural Cinderella story for class discussion:

- **Sowbellies**—fatty salt pork

- **Pigsty**—a muddy pen for pigs; sometimes used to describe a messy room or entire home.

- **Square-dance**—type of dancing for four couples arranged in a square with one couple facing each side and facing the middle of the square.

BluIz60/Shutterstock.com

Sootface: An Ojibwa Cinderella Story retold by Robert D. San Souci and illustrated by Daniel San Souci

Summary: Sootface, abused by her sisters, sang a hopeful song about someday finding a husband while she tended the fire. Sootface ignored the teasing of the entire town. Eventually, she mustered up the courage to dress herself in birch to go find a husband. She came across the hunter's sister in the forest and there she saw the hunter who was invisible to all the other women in the village. The hunter's sister washed away Sootface's imperfections and Sootface and the hunter were then married and lived happily ever after.

Unique words/phrases from this cultural Cinderella story for class discussion:

- **Bearers**—someone that carries/holds something

- **Moccasins**—soft leather slipper or shoe

- **Wigwam**—an American Indian dwelling

- **Deerskin skirt/robe**

- **Quillwork**—a type of decoration for clothing that uses soft and dyed porcupine or bird quills

Peter Turner Photography/Shutterstock.com

The Golden Sandal: A Middle Eastern Cinderella Story written by Rebecca Hickox and illustrated by Will Hillenbrand

Summary: Maha's stepmother was a hard woman to please. When things got tough, Maha would go to the river and the magic fish would help her out. The fish also granted Maha fine attire to wear with the bride's henna. As she rushed out of the merchant's house she left behind her golden sandal that was discovered by the bride's brother, Tariq. He went

Courtesy of T.D. Bazley

to search for Maha and they were married. As a humorous twist, Tariq's brother requested Maha's sister as a wife and as he lifted the veil to kiss her, all of her hair was replaced by blisters.

Unique words/phrases from this cultural Cinderella story for class discussion:

- **Henna**—tall bush or small tree

- **Bride's henna**—a dye made out of the henna plant used cosmetically for temporary tattooing for a bride.

- **Merchant**—a person that buys and sells different items

- **Hut**—a primitive dwelling

- **Betrothed**—engaged to be married

The Korean Cinderella written by Shirley Climo and illustrated by Ruth Heller

Summary: The Korean Cinderella is the story of Pear Blossom who lost her mother and was mistreated by her stepmother and stepsister. With the help of a magic frog and some helpful sparrows, Pear Blossom accomplished all that was asked of her but this still did not please her stepmother. The magistrate, captivated by Pear Blossom's beauty, called out to her when he saw her in the rice fields. Pear Blossom was startled and ran away leaving her straw slipper. The magistrate searched for her until they met and married.

Unique words/phrases from this cultural Cinderella story for class discussion:

- **Omoni**—mother

- **Hai**—the sun

- **Tokgabi**—goblin

- **Dried fish**—a preparation process for using fish as food

- **Pickled cabbage**—cabbage that is preserved in a sour liquid for food purposes

Chamille White/Shutterstock.com

beboy/Shutterstock.com

Courtesy of T.D. Bazley

- **Rice paddy field**—a watery/swampy plot of land for growing rice

- **Magistrate**—official officer of the state

- **Palanquin**—a passenger conveyance for a singular person

The Orphan: A Cinderella Story from Greece written by Anthony L. Manna and Soula Mitakidou and illustrated by Giselle Potter

Summary: The Orphan may have lost her mother but when she spoke to her mother's grave, she got an answer. The Orphan wept of all the misery her stepmother and stepsisters were causing and her mother told her not to worry and to return home. When the Orphan returned home Mother Nature and her children showered her with gifts that she stored away. The Prince attended church that Sunday and all the girls in attendance were hoping to catch his eye. Of course the Orphan, adorned in all her gifts, was the most beautiful but before the Prince could meet her, she fled. All he had was her shoe and he didn't rest soundly until he found her again. They were married and lived happily ever after.

Unique words/phrases from this cultural Cinderella story for class discussion:

- **Musk**—scented water.

- **Mother nature and her children**—sun, moon, dawn, morning star, evening star.

- **Sashayed**—glide or move easily.

The Persian Cinderella written by Shirley Climo and illustrated by Robert Florczak

Summary: Settareh's father gave all the women in the house some money to buy new cloths for Prince Mehrdad's festival. After smelling the delicious almonds, Settareh spent some of the money to sooth her grumbling stomach. Then, she came across a poor woman to whom she donated most of the money. Lastly, Settareh found a worn but beautiful blue pot that she spent the rest on. As it turns out, the tiny blue pot is magic and provided Settareh with the beautiful accessories she wanted for the festival. The Prince fell for Settareh but as they prepared for the wedding Settareh's stepsisters used her magic pot to put a curse on her to make her disappear using hairpins. As the Prince anxiously awaited for Settareh to return, he was comforted by a turtledove. The Prince noticed that the turtledove had hairpins stuck into it and removed them from the bird, revealing Settareh; thus breaking the curse.

Unique words/phrases from this cultural Cinderella story for class discussion:

- **Bazaar**—Middle Eastern Marketplace

- **Bleated**—sound from a sheep or goat

- **Merchants**—Sellers of goods

- **No Ruz**—The Persian New Year

- **Peddler**—someone who goes from place to place to sell goods

Courtesy of T.D. Bazley

Courtesy of T.D. Bazley

- **Cloak**—type of loose garment that is worn over clothing and protects the wearer from cold or rain

- **Jasmine blossoms**—a type of flower

- **Fragrance**—pleasant smell

- **Rhubarb**—thick leaf stalks that are red or green and can be eaten as a fruit after cooking them

- **Lute**—stringed instrument

- **Palanquin**—a passenger conveyance for a single person

- **Zither**—a musical instrument that is a flat wooden sound box with strings stretched across. It is used especially in folk music

- **Maiden**—unmarried girl

- **Turban**—a man's headdress

subin pumsom/Shutterstock.com

Jorg Hackemann/Shutterstock.com

The Rough-Face Girl written by Rafe Martin and illustrated by David Shannon

Summary: An Algonquin Indian version of Cinderella. The "Rough-Face Girl" was in charge of tending to the fire which left her skin and hair charred and dirty. Her older sisters laughed at her misfortune. Unlike her sisters, however, the Rough-Face Girl was able to see the most desired man in the village, the Invisible Being. The Invisible Being could see the beauty in her heart and they lived happily ever after.

Alexander Mazurkevich/Shutterstock.com

Unique words/phrases from this cultural Cinderella story for class discussion:

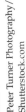

- **Wigwam**—hut

- **Buckskin**—a hair coat color of horses, similar to deerskin

- **Moccasins**—type of slipper or shoe made of soft leather originated by North American Indians

- **Dried reeds**—leaves from a type plant

- **Birch bark**—bark of several birch trees of the genus Betula

- **Raven**—a type of bird

The Salmon Princess: An Alaska Cinderella Story written and illustrated by Mindy Dwyer

Summary: Set in Southeast Alaska and full of figurative language (typical in Alaskan stories), *The Salmon Princess* is yet another unique twist on the classic Cinderella tale. After the death of Cinder's mother, her father remarried and her new stepmom gave Cinder the job of cleaning all of the fish. This was a messy job of course! With an eagle instead of a fairy godmother and the Silver Salmon Festival instead of a royal ball, Cinder meets the "prince" who is really just a boy from a well-known fishing family. After Cinder rushes off for her curfew, the boy finds her by following the sound of her song and freeing her from her brothers' hiding place.

Unique words/phrases from this cultural Cinderella story for class discussion:

- **Phosphorescent**—shining/gleaming

- **Smokehouse**—a structure where meat or fish is preserved with smoke

- **Salmon**—type of fish

Yeh-Shen: A Cinderella Story from China retold by Ai-Ling Louie and illustrated by Ed Young

wiktord/Shutterstock.com

Summary: Yeh-Shen's father had two wives. She grew up in her stepmother's home after her father and mother passed away from illness. The only happiness Yen-Shen experienced was the company of her pet fish that she shared her food with. The stepmother was spiteful and killed the fish for supper, which broke Yeh-Shen's heart. An old man appeared and told Yeh-Shen about the magic that the fish bones possessed. She gathered the bones of her fish and with this she wished for food. Yeh-Shen waited for the festival to wish for the luxuries of beautiful clothing and the fish granted her that, including gold slippers. Her stepsister recognized Yeh-Shen at the festival but before she could get a good look, Yeh-Shen ran away leaving a slipper behind. The King received the other slipper and became infatuated with it. He found Yeh-Shen to be the owner and they fell in love.

martiapunts/Shutterstock.com

CHAINFOTO24/Shutterstock.com

Unique words/phrases from this cultural Cinderella story for class discussion:

- **Dynasties**—a sequence of rulers from the same family

- **Sweetmeats**—any sweet delicacy or candy

- **Azure blue**—deep sky blue

- **Kingfisher feathers**—crested bird with a short tail and bright feathers

- **Vigil**—a time of staying awake when most people are sleeping, especially to keep watch or pray

While for the purposes of this book and in my own classroom I used the tale of Cinderella, you could choose another traditional literature tale that has different cultural variations as well and use the same ideas and suggestions.

Other Diverse Children's Literature

Following are summaries of other recommended children's literature for use in teaching diversity and multicultural education.

- *A Bike Like Sergio's* by Maribeth Boelts; illustrated by Noah Z. Jones

  Summary: This is a touching story about a little boy named Ruben who comes from a low socio-economic background. He really wants a new bike for his birthday but he knows "wishing for money won't make it appear." One day, he finds a $100 dollar bill and suddenly he sees a new bike in his future. The guilt and sadness he feels makes him question what to do. This book is relatable and relevant to young readers who may be struggling with doing the right thing.

- *A Day's Work* by Eve Bunting

  Summary: Francisco's grandfather just recently came to live in the United States when Francisco decided to help him find work. When a man approached them looking for gardeners, Francisco lied and told them they knew how to garden. "They'd just figure it out," he thought. When the man returned to see what Francisco and his grandfather had accomplished he was shocked to find that they had pulled the plants and left the weeds. Francisco's grandfather lectured him, in Spanish, about the importance of being honest and because of his apologetic demeanor and his hard work ethic the man agreed to hire the grandfather for more days of work after all.

- *Ada Twist, Scientist* by Andrea Beaty

  Summary: This is a captivating story about Ada Twist, a little girl with a head full of questions. When her experiments get out of hand, her parents banish her to the "thinking chair." Will this help Ada control her curious mind? Students will love this follow up to *Rosie Revere, Engineer* and *Iggy Peck, Architect* as Andrea Beaty continues to write catchy poems and fun stories that inspire children to pursue their passions.

- *And Tango Makes Three* by Justin Richardson and Peter Parnell

Courtesy of Kristen Bazley

Summary: A true story that illustrates that even in the animal world a family can be comprised of two males, and not necessarily just a male and a female. At the Central Park Zoo, two male penguins formed a pair bond and were inseparable. The two males saw the other penguin families nesting their eggs, and followed suit sitting on stones they gathered. A zoo employee saw their activities and had an idea. The zoo had fertilized an egg that another penguin family could not nurture. He placed the egg in the two males' nest. After a few weeks, the two male penguins were penguin dads.

- *Arctic Aesop's Fables* by Susi Gregg Fowler

Twelve of Aesop's Fables retold with an arctic animal and an arctic environs backdrop.

- *Beatrice's Goat* by Page McBrier

Summary: When Beatrice's family received a donated goat, she had no idea how much it would help the family. She took good care of the goat and, sure enough, the goat gave birth twice, provided the family with milk to drink and sell, and Beatrice was even able to attend school with the money they made! Who knew something as small as a goat could bring such big things!

- *Be the Change: A Grandfather Gandhi Story* by Arun Gandhi and Bethany Hegedus illustrated by Evan Turk

Summary: This is a story of Arun Gandhi, Gandhi's grandson, as he learns to live a life of simplicity, nonviolence, and the 11 vows of Ashram living. The boy learns many lessons from watching his grandfather speak to thousands of people. This is the personal story of the way Gandhi helped his grandson learn the connection between violence and living without waste. Arun learns that the every wasteful act affects others. The book teaches its readers one of Gandhi's most valuable lessons about how to *Be the Change*.

- *Cheyenne Again* by Eve Bunting

Summary: An historical fiction tale about a young Cheyenne boy taken from his family and forced to attend a boarding school for Indians. This story shows how insensitive America was to the culture of Native Americans at that time and how far it went to strip them of this culture. The young boy misses his home and his family, and ultimately his Cheyenne culture. As he draws a picture of Cheyenne warriors on horseback he is drawn back to his native culture and is "Cheyenne again."

Courtesy of T.D. Bazley

Courtesy of T.D. Bazley

- *Chik Chak Shabbat* by Mara Rockliff

  Summary: Although this story focuses on the Jewish culture, it also highlights sharing food as an easy and generous way for people of different backgrounds to come together. In *Chik Chak Shabbat*, everyone in the apartment building looks forward to smelling Goldie's cholent for Shabbat. Shabbat is a day of rest and the family usually prepares food ahead of time so that the day is relaxing. One week, the neighbors do not smell the cholent and Goldie explains she was too sick. All the neighbors from various cultures all come together and bring their family's signature dish to celebrate Shabbat together.

- *Dear Dragon* by Josh Funk; illustrated by Rodolfo Montalvo

  Summary: This is a story about diversity and friendship. George and Blaise are pen pals. They write poems to each other as part of a class project. Their friendship begins to grow, but things aren't always what they seem to be. When the pen pals meet at the end of the year they are in for a BIG surprise!

- *Dinner at Aunt Connie's House* by Faith Ringgold

  Summary: The paintings at Aunt Connie's house are anything but ordinary. Lonnie and Melody learn all about the Civil Rights Movement from the talking paintings that hang in Aunt Connie's house. The painting of Rosa Parks tells the story of the Montgomery Bus Boycott. Fannie Lou Harmer and several other women  of the Civil Rights movements tell their stories as well. Dinner at Aunt Connie's House reminds Americans of our past and how hard people had to fight for the freedoms we enjoy today.

Courtesy of Kristen Bazley

- *Esperanza Rising* by Pan Munoz Ryan

  Summary: Born into a privileged family in Mexico, Esperanza lived a happy, carefree life. When Esperanza's father is murdered, she and her mother have no choice but to flee to the United States. America, in midst of the Great Depression, a move that has its own struggles. Esperanza has to face adversity and care for her mother in this coming-of-age story.

- *Everybody Bakes Bread* by Norah Dooley

  Summary: As Carrie travels the neighborhood looking to borrow a three-handled rolling pin for her grandmother to bake Italian bread, she meets all types of families and they are all baking bread too! Every family bakes a different bread, and as Carrie samples each one, readers get a feel for each family and the culture all around them.

- *Giraffes Can't Dance* by Giles Andreae

  Summary: Gerald feels left out as he watches all the other animals dance together. Gerald could not dance with his crooked knees like the lions could. Each animal pair did a different dance: tango, the waltz, the cha-cha, and so on. It was not until a wise cricket offered advice that Gerald realized what he was missing. All he needed was the right music. With the music of the cricket, Gerald danced his heart out to the surprise of all his animal friends. The use of rhyme, rhythm, and alliteration make this book a great read aloud in the classroom.

- *Grandmother's Dreamcatcher* by Becky Ray McCain; illustrated by Stacey Schuett

  Summary: Kimmy is a little girl who will be spending a week with her grandmother while her parents search for a new house to live in. Kimmy misses her parents and is worried because she has been having bad dreams. Her grandmother is Chippewa and decides to teach her about the legend of dreamcatchers. The warm, descriptive writing and whimsical pictures take the reader right back to the comfort of a grandmother's love and provides a hands-on solution to ending bad dreams. This is an example of a book that can be used to incorporate the Native American culture into lessons.

- *Grandpa, Is Everything Black Bad?* by Sandy Lynne Holman

  Summary: This powerful story aims to let everyone know that not everything that is black is bad. The grandfather in this story reveals the impact of heritage and the importance the elderly have on the youth of a culture. The illustrations and the story reflect that self-love is important for everyone to understand the real purpose of equality, to understand that we are all special, unique, and great human beings.

- *Iggy Peck, Architect* by Andrea Beaty

  Summary: This is a story about a little boy who loves to build. He enjoys building larger than life replicas of iconic buildings around the world. With the help of his encouraging teacher, Iggy Peck learns the powerful lessons of diversity, individuality, and perseverance.

- *Imogene's Last Stand* by Candace Fleming and Nancy Carpenter

  Summary: In this nonfiction book, Imogene loves history and her beloved small town of Liddleville. One day, she hears that her town's Historical Society is being torn down and replaced with a shoelace factory. Imogene takes girl-power to the next level when she refurbishes the whole building by herself and fights to keep the Historical Society alive. Drawing from inspirational quotes said throughout history, this book inspires its readers to fight for what they love and never give up.

Courtesy of Kristen Bazley

- *In Andal's House* by Gloria Whelan

  Summary: "We light the lamps of Diwali to drive away the darkness of ignorance." *In Andal's House* is a short yet powerful coming of age story about a boy living in India. This book teaches children about the caste system and the progress India has made thus far. Packed with cultural references, Whelan writes about Kumar's experience of having his sister sacrifice her dreams so he can achieve his family's expectations, the customs of the Diwali holiday, and the discrimination he faces from older generations that still judge people based on their caste.

- *In Jesse's Shoes: Appreciating Kids with Special Needs* by Beverly Lewis

  Summary: A tender look at what it is like to live with special needs children. Allie knows her brother, Jesse, is different; her dad says he is "wired differently." At times Allie has trouble coming to terms with his "odd" behaviors, even though she truly loves her brother. As she walks him to his bus stop, she has to find the courage and words to deal with other kids who are laughing and commenting about her brother's odd behavior. Her dad tells her that she should walk in his shoes to understand him. One day Jesse asks her to put on his shoes and look at the world as he does and she finally and truly understood her brother.

- *In My Family* by Carmen Lomas Garza

  Summary: *In My Family* is written in side-by-side English and Spanish. Carmen Lomas Garza includes a personal note in the beginning that explains why art is so important to her and the struggles she and her family had to maintain their Mexican culture. This book is a collection of stories that make up the author's culture. She passes down these heartfelt and educational family memories and stories to readers.

- *Just Plain Fancy* by Patricia Polacco

  Summary: Naomi is a young, Amish girl, who wishes she had something fancy. One day she finds a spotted egg in the chicken coop. She cares for the egg and when it hatches, the bird is not like the other chickens. When Naomi learns about shaming in the Amish culture, she fears that "Fancy," the unique bird, will be shamed. She hides him away until he surprisingly makes an appearance to the family and their friends. Luckily, everyone loves Fancy and Naomi earns her white cap for taking such good care of him.

- *Lead Us to Freedom, Harriet Tubman!* by Peter and Connie Roop

    Summary: Harriet Tubman led slaves on the Underground Railroad in search of freedom. This book, however, tells readers of her life prior to her legacy. Born a slave, Harriet dreamt of a better life. Her life as a slave was full of harsh memories but Harriet remained hopeful and took action.

- *Light the Lights* by Margaret Mooreman

    Summary: Emma loves the winter holidays. They make the winter nights not seem so dark. Her family takes turns lighting the menorah each night and eats traditional Jewish foods, like latkes. Emma's family also sets up a Christmas tree and receives presents from Santa. This story describes how fun these holidays can be, especially for a family that celebrates both Hanukkah and Christmas.

- *Malala's Magic Pencil* by Malala Yousafzai; illustrated by Kerascoet

    Summary: Malala is now a Nobel Peace Prize winner for her dedication to education for girls in Pakistan and around the world. She was once a little girl who longed for a magic pencil to create a better place for her family and community. As the story describes, Malala grew tired of hoping for something impossible and out of reach. She set out to create her own magic by writing about the dangers of the world around her. People began to listen. Today, people from all over the world have read her letters and listened to her speak. This children's book teaches its young readers to be strong and dedicated to what you believe in.

Courtesy of Kristen Bazley

- *Maya Lin: Artist-Architect of Light and Lines Designer of the Vietnam Veteran's Memorial* by Jeanne Walker Harvey; illustrated by Dow Phumiruk

  Summary: Maya Lin grew up in rolling hills she named the Lizard's Back. She loved to explore the forest, looking for animals and observing nature. At home, her mother was a poet and her father was an artist. She loved to play with her brother. Together they watched as their parents breathed life in to their creations. Maya dreamed of becoming an architect. When Maya Lin heard of the Vietnam Memorial contest, she knew she had to enter. This is a story of embracing who you are and never giving up on your dreams.

- *My Name Is Bilal* by Asma Mobin-Uddin

  Summary: When Bilal and his sister Ayesha arrive at a new school, Bilal is sure that he and Ayesha are the only Muslim kids around. He watches as boys make fun of his sister in her traditional Muslim clothes. He wants to fit in. With the help of his Muslim teacher, he learns to accept his culture and adapt to his new school. This story of diversity and acceptance is relevant for all students in every school in the United States.

- *My Name Is Maria Isabel* by Alma Flor Ada

  Summary: What if one day your teacher decided to change your name? This is exactly what happens to Maria. Maria feels like she has lost part of herself. Why should she be the "Maria" in class that has to change her name? Readers get a sense of Maria's lost pride when she loses her name and her greatest wish is getting it back.

- *Nasreen's Secret School: A True Story From Afghanistan* by Jeanette Winter

  Summary: This book is based on a true story from Afghanistan. One night, a young girl's father was carried away by soldiers and when he did not return, her mother left to try and find him. However, it was forbidden for women and girls to go out alone on the streets and her mother did not return. The young girl stops speaking and smiling and waits for her parents to return. In the meantime, her grandmother decides to enroll her granddaughter in a small secret school for girls in hopes that finding a new friend and the world of education would help her granddaughter overcome the tragedy and loss she has faced.

- *Nelson Mandela* by Kadir Nelson

  Summary: The inspiring true story of the life of Nelson Mandela who saw injustice in his home country of South Africa in the oppressive apartheid system and fought to change it. He became a lawyer and fought for social change. He was imprisoned for nearly three decades for his beliefs in social change. When the apartheid system was finally abandoned, Nelson was released from prison and eventually became the first black president of South Africa.

- *Nine O'Clock Lullaby* by Marilyn Singer

  Summary: Marilyn Singer takes readers all over the world in *Nine O'Clock Lullaby*. The book starts at 9 P.M. in Brooklyn, NY and then brings the reader to Puerto Rico where, because of the time difference, it is 10 p.m. The words and illustrations enlighten readers to all sorts of cultures, before returning back to Brooklyn.

- *Not So Different: What You Really Want to Ask about Having a Disability* by Shane Burcaw

  Summary: This is a story by a boy named Shane who is living with muscular dystrophy, a disease that affects the way his body grows and functions. The author wrote this book to answer common questions about his life. He wants people to know that even though he needs a lot of help, he is not so different.

- *Number the Stars* written by Lois Lowry

  Summary: Annemarie is trying to make sense of war in this novel set in the time of the Holocaust. This family's life is full of hardship and secrecy but there is also hope—the Danish Resistance. Annemarie's parents, Mr. and Mrs. Johanson, take in a Jewish

fuyu liu/Shutterstock.com

girl, named Ellen. Ellen assumes the identity of Annemarie's oldest sister who died earlier in the war and the family struggles to conceal her real identity from the soldiers' constant presence.

- *One Hen: How One Small Loan Made a Big Difference* by Katie Smith Milway

  Summary: This is the story of how a young boy named Kojo, turned a small loan from village families, after his father died, to help his mom on the farm. He bought one brown hen, which not only helped the family but also the community, and country. This was based on a true story from Ghana.

- *Rechenka's Eggs* by Patricia Polacco

  Summary: Babushka paints the most beautiful eggs in Moskva. One day, she found an injured goose, Rechenka, in her yard and brings it inside to nurse back to health. The goose, in return, lays an egg every morning for Babushka to eat for breakfast. Before Babushka could take her prize-winning eggs to the Easter Festival, Rechenka accidentally crushes all of the eggs and spills her paint. Rechenka knew she had upset Babushka and began laying eggs even more beautiful and colorful than the hand-painted ones. Rechenka had to fly north but she left one more surprise for Babushka, a gosling of her own, born from a beautiful egg.

- *Rosie Revere, Engineer* by Andrea Beaty; illustrated by David Roberts

  Summary: Rosie Revere is a little girl who loved to build. She often rummaged through the trash in search of materials and worked late into the night on her inventions. She made these inventions for family and friends. The story captivates its audience with its witty story and catchy rhymes and would be great to use in the classroom to encourage diversity and individuality.

- *Rube Goldberg's Simple Normal Humdrum School Day* by Jennifer George

  Summary: Rube is a boy who is anything but ordinary. Rube's important mission is to make everything in his life easier, but for Rube, when up is down and in is out, even the most easy daily tasks become complex! This is a cute and humorous story that emphasizes creativity and diversity.

- *Ruby Bridges Goes to School: My True Story* by Ruby Bridges

  Summary: Full of vivid, historical photos, *Ruby Bridges Goes to School* tells the true story of a young African American girl who attended a white school during the desegregation era in the U.S. This story shows the bravery Ruby Bridges exhibited and opposition that she faced at such a young age.

- *Ruby's Chinese New Year* by Vickie Lee; illustrated by Joey Chou

  Summary: Every year Ruby spends the Chinese New Year with her grandmother but this year her grandmother cannot travel. Ruby decides to bring the Chinese New Year to her grandmother! She sets off on a journey with a picture she made for her grandmother. On her way, she meets all 12 zodiac animals and they all celebrate together in a magical story that represents the legend of the Chinese Zodiac.

Courtesy of T.D. Bazley

- *Schomburg: The Man Who Built a Library* by Carole Boston Weatherford; illustrated by Eric Velasquez

  Summary: Arturo Schomburg was an Afro-Puerto Rican man who lived during the Harlem Renaissance in New York City. He believed in the importance of learning and preserving African American history for future generations. He lived his life collecting rare artifacts that became a beacon for the people of Harlem and all around the world. This book uses poetry to describe the life and struggles of Arturo, as well as his love of literature and the many ways African American people made a positive impact in our history.

- *So Far from the Sea* by Eve Bunting

  Summary: Laura's family walks through the desolate Manzanar War Relocation Camp as her father retells painful memories about World War II. Although the family has moved on and is moving away, the death of Laura's grandfather and her dad's stolen childhood are a sad part of their identity.

- *Suki's Kimono* by Chieri Uegaki

Summary: Suki's Kimono is a heartwarming story filled with culture about a girl who wears her kimono to school despite her sister's advice not to. Initially, Suki is teased but after she tells the class of her family and the street festival where she got it.

- *The Bat Boy and His Violin* by Gavin Curtis

Summary: Reginald is a boy who loves to play music on his violin. His father would rather he played baseball. Reginald is the batboy for his father's baseball team, the Dukes, the worst team in the Negro National League. Reginald begins to play his violin in the dugout and magical things begin to happen. It is a story about acceptance and diversity.

- *The Can Man* by Laura E. Williams

Summary: Tim's birthday is about a week away and knowing that money is scarce in the family, he decides to find and recycle cans in order to save money to buy a skateboard he really wants. As he collects his cans, he encounters a man that used to live in his building that is now homeless, due to losing his job. This man collects cans as well to survive and tells Tim that he is planning on using his can money to get a better coat for the winter. Throughout the story Tim learns valuable lessons about giving back, kindness, and empathy.

- *The First Strawberries: A Cherokee Story* retold by Joseph Bruchac

Summary: A Cherokee legend about how the first strawberries came into the world. The legend begins with a Cherokee husband and wife who had a fight. The man came home expecting dinner but the wife was picking flowers. The man had angry words with the woman and the woman left the man. The woman walked too fast and the man could not catch up to her. The sun could see the man regretted his angry words and took pity on him. The sun shone on the earth and put berries in the woman's path to slow her down. It was the strawberries that finally got the woman to stop and eat them and the man was able to catch up to her. The husband apologized for his angry words, and the wife shared her sweet strawberries with him. The sweet strawberries reminded her of their love for each other, and to this day this is how strawberries are symbolized in Cherokee culture.

- *The Hero and the Holocaust: The Story of Janusz Korczak and His Children* by David A. Adler

  Summary: *The Hero and the Holocaust* is a heartbreaking account of the life and legacy of Janusz Korczak. Janusz was recognized as a brilliant mind at a young age. He dedicated his life to children and opened an orphanage where he doctored the children and cared for them in every way. As the Nazis came to power in Germany, Janusz protested the anti-Semitic laws and found himself behind bars several times. In 1940, Korczak and all of the children he was caring for were forced into the Warsaw Ghetto and eventually killed in a concentration camp. Despite the ability of Janusz to leave the concentration camp, he followed the children he loved and sacrificed his own life.

- *The Journey* painting and text by Sheila Hamanaka; book design by Steve Frederick

  Summary: The story of racism and renewal is an elegant story with beautiful illustrations that tell of a very important part of American history: Japanese internment camps. The book describes the fear of Japanese immigrants after World War II. This book can be used in a social studies lesson to describe the lives of Americans after World War II.

- *The Matzah That Papa Brought Home* by Fran Manushkin

  Summary: Readers learn Jewish vocabulary and cultural traditions as Manushkin repeats the Passover activities. From "dipping our pinkies" to searching for the Afrikoman, *The Matzah That Papa Brought Home* is packed with culture and told in a way that children can read and repeat.

- *The Royal Bee* by Frances Park and Ginger Park

  Summary: There was no hope for Song-ho. He and his mother worked from dawn to dusk with little to show for it. He was born at a time in Korea where people of the lower class could not attend school. Song-ho longed to go to school but the closest he could get was outside the door. He would sit and listen to the teacher's lectures until the teacher relented and let him join the class. Subsequently, the class nominated Song-ho to go to the Royal Bee where he spoke of his struggles to the community and won the prize cow. The Royal Bee is a true underdog story about a boy motivated to make a better life for himself and his mother.

- *Throw Your Tooth on the Roof: Tooth Traditions from Around the World* by Selby B. Beeler

  Summary: Everyone loses their teeth at some point but you may be surprised to find out how different the traditions are all over the world. In the United States, we put our lost teeth under our pillows for the Tooth Fairy. This book tells of some unfamiliar, and maybe peculiar, tooth traditions.

- *To the Stars* by Carmella Van Vleet and Dr. Kathy Sullivan

  Summary: Kathy Sullivan was a little girl who loved to explore. She studied blueprints, and research on airplanes. She often had daydreams of getting on an airplane and going on an adventure! As she grew up, she learned foreign languages and enjoyed learning about different cultures. She wanted a job full of adventure. Despite the limitations of women during that time, Kathy Sullivan followed her heart and tried her best to learn as much as she could. She set out on a mission to see the world and eventually she did… from space!

- *We Are Shining* by Gwendolyn Brooks (Poetry)

  Summary: This poem is written for the children and families of the world. It is a story of acceptance, humanity, opportunity, equality, and love. The illustrations in this story show the beauty of diversity and hope in our world.

- *Yo Soy Muslim* by Mark Gonzales; illustrated by Mehrdokht Amini

Summary: Written in the form of a letter from a father to his daughter, this book is meant to explain the identity of growing up in a multicultural family. The story highlights the diversity of Spanish and Muslim cultures. The story is written with love and encourages its readers to learn about discovery and acceptance.

Supplemental Resources for Teaching Diversity and Multiculturalism through Children's Literature
Articles

- *Guiding Principles for Teaching Multicultural Literature* by Belinda Y. Louie

Kletr/Shutterstock.com

Summary: Checking materials for authenticity is a crucial step for educators to take, especially when teaching about culture. Louie goes on to give an array of texts that are authentic and perfect for use in diverse classrooms. With real-life classroom conversations, Louie presents this guide to multicultural literature with enough detail to make any educator confident to use these strategies in the classroom.

- Gunn, A. (2014). Honoring my students names! Using Web 2.0 tools to create culturally responsive literacy classrooms. *Childhood Education, 90*(2), 150–153.

Summary: Gunn writes about cases where students have been renamed by their teachers simply because their teacher could not pronounce their name. This article makes a case for the importance of personal identity. Gunn provides readers a classroom lesson that encourages students to explore their own cultural identity while also building an English vocabulary.

Useful Websites for Your Classroom

- **Cinderella:** http://www.pitt.edu/~dash/type0510a.html

  A variety of full-text, cultural Cinderella stories can be found on this website.

- **Cinderella Tales From Around the World:** http://www.lowvilleacademy.org/webpages/
  MBlow/cinderella.cfm?subpage=868111

  This website has free Cinderella literature from all over the world. There is also a great example
  of a classroom project, recording an audio book for one of the Cinderella tales.

- **Diversity Book Lists:** http://www.goodreads.com/list/tag/diversity

  This website has a list of books that identify with different diversities.

- **How to Choose the Best Multicultural Books:** http://www.scholastic.com/teachers/article/
  how-choose-best-multicultural-books

  This website provides teachers with tips and suggestions on how to choose appropriate multicultural books for the classroom.

- **Multicultural Cinderella Stories:** http://www.ala.org/offices/resources/multicultural

  This is another great resource for Cinderella stories from a variety of cultures.

References

Anderson, N. (2009). *Elementary children's literature: Infancy through age 13*. Upper Saddle River, NJ: Pearson.

Cole, R.W. (2008). Educating everybody's children: We know what works—and what doesn't. In R.W. Cole (Ed.). *Educating everybody's children: Diverse teaching strategies for diverse learners* (2nd ed.) (pp. 1–40). Arlington, VA: Association for Supervision and Curriculum Development.

Cruz, B., Ellerbrock, C. R., Vasquez, A., & Howes, E. V. (2014). *Talking diversity with teachers and teacher educators: Exercises and critical conversations across the curriculum*. New York, NY: Teachers College Press.

Dack, H., & Tomlinson, C. (2015). Inviting all students to learn. *Educational Leadership, 72*(6), 11–15.

Echevarria, J., Frey, N., & Fisher, D. (2015). What it takes for English learners to succeed. *Educational Leadership, 72*(6), 22–26.

Gonzalez-Mena, J. (2014). *50 strategies for communicating and working with diverse families* (3rd ed.). Upper Saddle River, NJ: Pearson

Irizarry, (2015). What Latino students want from school. *Educational Leadership, 72*(6), 66–71.

Johnson, D. (2015). The culturally proficient technologist. *Educational Leadership, 72*(6), 81–82.

Kovarik, M. (2014). Tell ELL's about culture. *New Teacher Advocate, 22*(1), 3._{A. LilesA. Liles}

English Language Learners/ English as a Second Language and Children's Literature

CLS Design/Shutterstock.com

While we have now considered how to use children's literature to enhance students' multicultural horizons, we've left one important group of students out of this discussion: those who are English language learners or more commonly, ELL students (or more rarely, Limited English Proficient (LEP) students) In most simple terms, these are students whose native language is not English but are in the process of learning English. Other definitions that have been put forth include:

- English language learners, or ELLs, are students who are unable to communicate fluently or learn effectively in English, who often come from non-English-speaking homes and backgrounds, and who typically require specialized or modified instruction in both the English language and in their academic courses (English-Language Learner Definition, 2013).

- Federal Definition of an English Language Learner (ELL): A national-origin-minority who is limited-English Proficient. This term is often preferred over limited English proficient (LEP) as it highlights accomplishments rather than deficits (US Department of Education, 2005).

In any case, it is important to distinguish the term ELL from another commonly used term, ESL, English as a second language. ESL refers to a program of techniques, methodology and special curriculum designed to teach ELL students English Language skills, which may include listening, speaking, reading, writing, study skills, content vocabulary and cultural orientation. ESL instruction is usually in English with little use of the native language. Thus, the distinction to be made here is that ELL refers to a student while ESL refers to a program.

Courtesy of T.D. Bazley

It is important to note that whatever definition you choose, the implications of not being fluent in English in a predominately. English-speaking classroom environment go beyond the obvious communication difficulties that non-English speaking students would encounter in achieving academic success. Many, if not most of these students, are usually recent immigrants to the United States, as well; which often means any English language deficit they may have, is often compounded by a cultural deficit, as well. Again, to put it simply, these are students who are not only non-English speakers but are also in a new land with unfamiliar customs and expectations; and their numbers in US classrooms are the most rapidly growing segment of the school-age population, bringing with them over 460 different languages (Planty et al., 2008). Thus, for some to say that we as educators have a huge challenge on our hands might be an understatement (e.g., see Zimmerman-Orozco, 2015). While ELL specialist teachers may need to work with ELL students to develop English language skills, all classroom teachers (especially those with ELL students) should strive to create a culturally inclusive classroom environment.

In this chapter, we explore how we can use children's literature to address the challenge of assisting ELL students in developing their English skills. In short, the same genres of children's literature that help to expand the cultural horizons of our native English-speaking students can assist ELL students in gaining English proficiency. Using books that have story themes

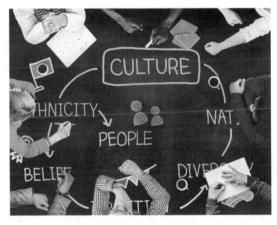

and settings that are culturally familiar to ELL students can provide the necessary enthusiasm and incentive to make progress in development of English skills.

Culture and the Classroom

My teaching career began in a public school second grade class of over 20 students and about half were English language learners. I was not surprised to find that Spanish was the first language for most of these ELL students and as a result of my undergraduate teacher education, I felt somewhat prepared to teach and work with these native Spanish-speakers. However, I also had a Vietnamese student, a Hungarian student, and a Bulgarian student, cultures and languages that presented new learning opportunities for me. Fortunately, for both these students and me, they were not reliant solely on their native languages, as they had already gained some English proficiency.

Stuart Miles/Shutterstock.com

However, cultural differences were noticeable to me, particularly with regard to the Vietnamese student. For example, whenever I would ask the students to form a line in order to walk outside, to another classroom, to an assembly, and so on, the entire class except this student would line up as directed. Only after asking this student individually to join the line would he do so. As this behavior continued, I sought the advice of a more experienced teacher who suggested I was encountering a cultural barrier; that is, it might be considered disrespectful to join a group unless specifically invited. Suddenly I realized that the problem at hand was more my lack of understanding this student's cultural background than this student being simply nonresponsive to my requests. Thus, on the one hand, I like many teachers, learned "on the job" the need to gain an understanding of the diverse cultures represented in my classroom in order to avoid misinterpreting behaviors of these students (Cole, 2008). Culturally responsive teachers create an environment that values diversity and builds on students' different ways of learning, behaving, and using language (Echevarria, Frey, & Fisher, 2015). However, on the other hand, it is also important for teachers to provide increasing awareness of classroom expectations and the mainstream culture where these students now reside (Kovarik, 2014).

Steps to Enhance Cultural Inclusiveness for ELL Students

More than ever, teachers need to become "world-wise," that is, they need to acquire a broad knowledge of the world's history, geography, literature, and so on; as well as skills in one or more languages other than English. Yes, a tall order, but undergraduate education students usually have to fulfill general education requirements

CHRISTIAN DE ARAUJO/Shutterstock.com

as part of their degree programs. So, choose wisely, get to know the world, and view this type of coursework as an essential part of your teacher preparation program. Why? Because, you need to have some knowledge of where your students are from, in order to create a culturally inclusive classroom. What are their customs and traditions? Did any of these children suffer traumatic experiences in their immigration journeys (Zimmerman-Orozco, 2015)? Even if you never received any formal instruction on a particular country

Blend Images/Shutterstock.com

or culture that is represented in your classroom, you can educate yourself through reading, through following current events from that part of the world, and through other forms of media including videos and the Internet. Echevarria, et al. (2015) caution that culturally diverse students who are chronically disengaged report that they lack positive relationships with teachers and are aware of disrespect toward their culture or ethnicity.

Courtesy of T.D. Bazley

Once in the classroom, teachers can send home a questionnaire to all families to gain familiarity in students' culture, traditions, and languages spoken within the family, and so on. Parent questionnaires can also be used to gather information on a student's talents, family expectations of the student, any translator needs, and times that would be convenient for school events or conferences. Accompanying these questionnaires can be pertinent information that all families should know about the school and classroom (Burnett, 2014).

Keep in mind, however, that any communication to the families of ELL students might need to be translated into the language(s) used in their homes. Absent the availability of school translator services, using online translation software such as found in *Google Docs (Translate Document)* can often make the difference between some ability to provide written communication with non-English–speaking parents versus none at all, if English is the only language when attempting to communicate with the homes of ELL students.

In the classroom, teachers should acquire basic phrases in any of the languages spoken by ELL students. For students who lack any facility with English being able to ask questions in their language about essential needs such as use of a bathroom, request for water or feeling ill is of obvious importance. In addition, for those ELL students whose native language is not shared by any other student in the classroom, at least the teacher is making some attempt to establish a common ground for communication and thus striving for greater cultural inclusiveness in the classroom. While many teachers may have some knowledge of Spanish through prior coursework or simply acquired it through exposure to our increasingly dual language (i.e., English/Spanish) society, they are less likely to be familiar with the languages of other prominent immigrant groups such as those from Asia and the Middle East. In these instances, teachers will need to take the initiative to acquire basic words, phrases, and so on, much like the efforts necessary to become familiar with the culture and customs that students from these areas bring into their classrooms.

Another step for creating cultural inclusiveness in the class is to encourage ELL students to share their culture and traditions, to include their language. Asking students how to say certain words in their native language shows cultural respect (Echevarria et al., 2015) and helps to encourage them to maintain fluency in their native language while learning English (Irizarry, 2015; Olsen, 2010).

Likewise, having on display in the classroom, an array of visuals in both English and the languages of the ELL students helps to establish a culturally inclusive classroom environment. Moreover, such visuals are learning aids for ELL students because objects are associated with words, an important process in vocab-

Tupungato/Shutterstock.com

ulary and reading comprehension development (DeAngelo, 2014; Segal, 2014). To learn specific phrases or vocabulary, I have found that using *Google Translate* works well.

Another one of my favorite steps for creating a culturally inclusive classroom is "buddy-pairing" for ELL students. ELL students from similar cultural and language backgrounds can often benefit from being paired together for some classroom activities (e.g., paired reading and other collaborative learning activities [Cole, 1995]), especially when one has a better facility with English than the other.

iofoto/Shutterstock.com

Moreover, some English-speaking students may enjoy being paired with ELL students to help them along in the classroom and the school, generally, even if a language barrier exists. These kinds of arrangements can ease transitions into the classroom for ELL students, both socially and academically. In fact, Olsen (2010) touts the value of ELL students learning among diverse students. Not surprisingly, this may be an excellent learning experience for the English-speaking student as well, in terms of establishing a relationship with a student from a different culture and speaking a different language.

What Doesn't Work or What to Avoid

While the above section contained recommendations for enhancing the cultural inclusiveness for ELL students, teachers should also be aware of the "don'ts" when dealing with ELL students and/or creating cultural inclusiveness in the classroom. Although we've stressed the need for teachers to be culturally conscious and educated, it's equally important not to generalize a culture to each individual student from that background. First and foremost, teachers need to view each student as an individual with a unique personality, talents, needs, aspirations, and interests, and their educational experience should be tailored accordingly (Dack & Tomlinson, 2015). Within this framework, however, a student's culture need not be ignored either, such as insisting that only English be spoken in the classroom. During free time/social time in the classroom, teachers should allow students to converse in their native language(s) (Gandara, 2015). Conversely, don't assume that just because an ELL student has facility with English, that his/her parents will, as well. As discussed above, written communications going to homes of ELL students should be translated into the student's native language(s). Burnett (2014) cautions against depending upon students to translate for their families. Doing so could be especially problematic in the context of parent/teacher conferences.

Group work can be challenging for ELL students if they feel their contributions are not being recognized (DeAngelo, 2014). The practice of pairing an ELL student with another student to work together on class and instructional activities as discussed above may be a good segue to participation in group work. Finally, don't assume an "OK" or nod of the head confirms

Rawpixel/Shutterstock.com

Marcos Mesa Sam Wordley/Shutterstock.com

understanding when trying to gauge ELL student learning. Likewise, DeAngelo urges teachers of ELL students to avoid "Yes"/"No" questions to check for understanding as it is "too easy" to just answer "Yes," without really having any basis for that answer.

Children's Literature: How It Helps ELL Students

Children's literature allows the teacher to help the ELL students understand the world around them using picture books. For example, in a unit about the ocean, a teacher can bring in picture books to enhance the student's knowledge about the ocean. Get books about different cultures so that all students can learn about a variety of cultures and students of different cultures feel included in the classroom environment. Students also learn about diversity through the use of different books, which enhances their understanding of each other, their backgrounds, where they lived, what they like to eat, and so on. Have students share photographs from their homeland. Krashen (2004) is a strong proponent of free voluntary reading as it helps ELL learners dramatically by increasing comprehension and vocabulary. Krashen also has stated that time devoted to teaching vocabulary lists is better spent doing free voluntary reading because students are more likely to improve their word acquisition. Krashen has further

stated that developing literacy in their first language is the key to develop literacy in a new language and students who read for pleasure in their heritage language have better retention of that language than students who don't.

szefei/Shutterstock.com

Courtesy of T.D. Bazley

Listed below are some recommended children's literature books that span a variety of cultures and that would be enjoyable reading for your ELL students as well your English-speaking students.

Courtesy of T.D. Bazley

Suggested Children's Literature to Include in Your Classroom and in Your Lessons

- *Apple Pie 4th of July* by Janet S. Wong

  Summary: *Apple Pie 4th of July* is about a girl who works with her family at their Chinese restaurant. She complains how the restaurant is open on every holiday except Christmas and that she is missing out on American traditions. Surprisingly, the restaurant fills with customers as the hours get later and then she gets to enjoy apple pie and fireworks.

wavebreakmedia/Shutterstock.com

- *Chinatown* by William Low

  Summary: William Low's words and illustrations capture the sights, smells, and sounds of Chinatown like no other. Readers will discover what is happening in Chinatown or maybe what *isn't* happening in Chinatown. Low is able to convey a feeling of the energy that is Chinatown.

Lyudmyla Kharlamova/Shutterstock.com

- *From the Bellybutton of the Moon* by Francisco X. Alarcon

  Summary: Written in side-by-side English and Spanish, *From the Bellybutton of the Moon is* a collection of poems that bring nature and Mexican culture alive.

- *I Hate English* by Ellen Levine

  Summary: Nostalgic about her native language, Chinese, Mei Mei struggles to learn English at her new school. Mei Mei resents the fact that she's being forced to learn a new language. The teacher spends a lot of time building a relationship with Mei Mei (in English) and eventually Mei Mei realizes that she wants to participate in the conversation and "accidentally" begins speaking English. This story captures the reluctance some ELL students may have at first and illustrates some ways to motivate students to become more fluent in English.

- *I Love Saturdays y Domingos* by Alma Flor Ada

  Summary: *I Love Saturdays y Domingos* is a story of a little girl who has two different cultures that make up her personal identity.

Courtesy of T.D. Bazley

- *My Diary from Here to There* by Amada Irma Perez

  Summary: A young girl from Mexico shares her feelings as her father goes to United States to look for work. The story goes back and forth showing the similarities and differences that this little girl experiences. This book is written so that readers can use context to learn how to say words in Spanish.

- *My Name Is SANGOEL* by Karen Lynn Williams and Khadra Mohammed

  Summary: A refugee often has to leave home spontaneously. This was the case for Sangoel and his family. When Sangoel's family came from Sudan and settled in United States, they had to learn simple things like how to cook on the stove and how to dial a telephone. *My name is Sangoel* is the story of a boy who loses his father in Sudan and must come to United States, assimilate, and be the man of the house.

- *My Name Is Yoon* by Helen Recorvits

  Summary: *My Name Is Yoon* takes readers inside the mind of a little girl who is resisting writing her name in English. She would rather write anything else, but she likes her name in Korean. As Yoon gains more positive experiences in United States, she decides to write her name and comes to terms with the fact that it still carries the same meaning: shining wisdom.

- *My Very Own Room* by Amada Irma Perez

  Summary: Written in side-by-side English and Spanish, *My Very Own Room* is about a girl who lives in a very chaotic house. She already has a large family but other family members from Mexico often come to stay as well. Eventually, she convinces her mother to allow her to make a room out of a storage area in the house. This story is about appreciation and making something out of nothing.

- *No English* by Jacqueline Jules

  Summary: In *No English*, a story of cultural miscommunication unfolds as a new student from Argentina, Blanca, joins Diane's class. At first, Diane offends Blanca as she tried to interact and Blanca does not understand. Eventually, the two girls set an example for how to welcome a student who is learning English—they draw pictures to communicate.

- *Tea with Milk* by Allen Say

  Summary: Masako's parents were from Japan but they raised her in the United States. Masako found comfort in the American culture but her parents decided to move back to Japan when she finished high school. Masako refused

Courtesy of T.D. Bazley

to conform to the traditional expectations of her parents and she went to work in the city where she could make a living, speaking English. It was there where she met her fiancé and discovered that home is not always a place.

- *Too Many Tamales* by Gary Soto

  Summary: *Too Many Tamales* is a Christmas story that describes a family's tradition of making tamales. The story includes Spanish vocabulary as the family cooks and includes a humorous story of the kids looking for the mother's ring by eating *way too many* tamales.

  Riccardo Mayer/Shutterstock.com

- *The Upside Down Boy: El nino de cabeza* by Juan Felipe Herrera

  Summary: This is the author's story of a teacher who made a difference. Juan, the author, began school knowing little, to no English. He felt weird, even a little "upside-down", in school at first. His teacher, Mrs. Sampson, tells him he has a beautiful singing voice and gives him A's on his poetry assignments. With all this encouragement, Juan is noticeably happier and more confident.

Supplemental Resources for Teaching Diversity and Multiculturalism through Children's Literature
Articles

- Pang, Y. (2013). Graphic organizers and other visual strategies to improve young ELLs' reading comprehension. *The NERA Journal*, *48*(2), 52–58.

  Summary: Pang insists that reading is the foundation of learning for English language learners. This article includes several useful visual tools that increase students' comprehension as well as suggested children's books to use in the classroom.

- Dong, Y. (2013). Powerful learning tools for ELLs: Using native language familiar examples, and concept mapping to teach English language learners. *The Science Teacher, 80*(4), 51–57.

Summary: After warning educators about cultural misperceptions they may have, Dong provides easy-to-integrate activities that help to teach English language learners. By incorporating students' prior knowledge, concept mapping goes farther than teaching single-word vocabulary and teaches relationships among concepts.

- Bautista, N., & Castañeda, M. (2011). Teaching science to ELLs, part 1: Key strategies every science teacher should know. *The Science Teacher, 78*(3), 35–39.

Summary: Directed toward science teachers but useful for any educator, Bautista, and Castañeda provide specific planning strategies for teachers of ELL students. Starting with knowing each student's proficiency level, educators should align content and language objectives and create links from content to the student's background knowledge. This article is the first of a series that give step-by-step suggestions for teacher's who want all of their students to be successful.

- Carger, C., & Koss, M. (2014). "Getting to know you": Using ABC books to develop vocabulary and exchange cultural information with English language learners. *Illinois Reading Council Journal, 42*(4), 11–18.

Summary: Connecting classroom content to students' background knowledge is essential when teaching ELL students. Carger and Koss offer specific ABC books that could be used in the classroom. As ELL students develop vocabulary, the authors suggest having students making ABC books of their own and provide classroom examples of this.

Useful Websites

Andresr/Shutterstock.com

- **Colorin Colorado:** A bilingual site for families and educators of English language learners. http://www.colorincolorado.org/ This website includes webcasts that keep teachers up to date on the best educational practices for ELL students. Colorin Colorado is also useful for families and provides tips for what parents can do to help their child succeed. The book lists are categorized so that educators, parents, and students can search for materials that best relate to their own culture or learn about the cultures of others.

- **Top Ten Websites for ESL Teacher:** http://busyteacher.org/7054-top-10-websites-esl-teacher/html The Busy Teacher website has free worksheets, flashcards, and teaching ideas and on top of that, they have compiled a list of nine other websites that are great for ESL educators. From grammar and vocabulary building to video quizzes and teaching materials, these websites cover all the bases that make a successful, ESL-friendly classroom.

- **Starfall: Learn to Read with Phonics:** http://www.starfall.com

Starfall is learner friendly from the start. With an easy-to-navigate website, Starfall starts with the ABC's and builds reading skills through 4 levels: ABCs, Learn To Read, It's Fun to Read, and I'm Reading. Students "learn to read" with a variety of games, easy-to-read texts, and videos. Once children learn the basics of phonics, Starfall even fosters reading appreciation by offering diverse texts from all sorts of genres.

- **ESL Point:** http://www.eslpoint.com

  ESL Point is a website organized by skills: speaking, listening, grammar, pronunciation, business, writing, reading, vocabulary, TOEFL (English language test), and idioms. Whether you're an educator or a student, ESL Point easily navigates you to the materials you're looking for! Each skill area is broken down into skill level as well putting quizzes, web links, and recommended textbooks right at your fingertips.

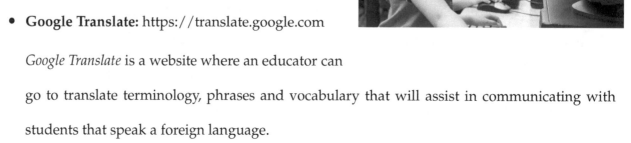

- **Google Translate:** https://translate.google.com

  Google Translate is a website where an educator can go to translate terminology, phrases and vocabulary that will assist in communicating with students that speak a foreign language.

Monkey Business Images/ Shutterstock.com

Ten ELL Terms Educators Should Know*

1. **Bilingual:** The ability to communicate proficiently in two languages.

2. **Collaborative ESL Programs:** These are programs in which ESL specialists collaborate with mainstream teachers to provide instruction to ELLs.

3. **Culture Shock:** The feeling of uncertainty when someone is exposed to a drastically different and unfamiliar environment.

4. **Dual-Language Programs:** Instruction is given in two different languages.

5. **Language Acquisition:** The informal learning of a language through experience.

6. **L1:** A person's first language, also known as their native language.

7. **L2:** A person's second language, or the nonnative language. For ELLs, their second language is English.

8. **Pullout ESL Programs:** These are programs in which the ESL student is pulled out of a mainstream classroom for individualized ESL instruction.

9. **Sheltered English Instruction (SEI):** A teaching approach that is used to make instruction in English more understandable for ELLs.

10. **Silent Period:** This is the first phase of a new language acquisition. It is when ELLs are unable or unwilling to speak in their new language.

*Resources for the above, which are also listed in in the reference section:

Cole, R.W. (2008). Educating everybody's children: We know what works—and what doesn't. In R.W. Cole (Ed.), *Educating everybody's children: Diverse teaching strategies for diverse learners* (2nd ed., pp. 1–40). Arlington, VA: Association for Supervision and Curriculum Development.

English-Language Learner Definition. (2013, August 19). Retrieved from http://edglossary.org/ englishlanguage-learner

References

Burnett, C. G. (2014). Opening the door to family involvement. *New Teacher Advocate*, 22(1), 4–5.

Cole, R.W. (2008). Educating everybody's children: We know what works—and what doesn't. In R.W. Cole (Ed.), *Educating everybody's children: Diverse teaching strategies for diverse learners* (2nd ed., pp. 1–40). Arlington, VA: Association for Supervision and Curriculum Development.

Dack, H., & Tomlinson, C. (2015). Inviting all students to learn. *Educational Leadership*, 72(6), 11–15.

DeAngelo, M. W. (2014). 5 guidelines to support culturally transitioning students. *New Teacher Advocate*, 22(1), 8–9.

Echevarria, J., Frey, N., & Fisher, D. (2015). What it takes for English learners to succeed. *Educational Leadership*, *72*(6), 22–26.

English-Language Learner Definition. (2013, August 19). Retrieved from http://edglossary.org/english-language-learner

Gandara, P. (2015). Rethinking bilingual instruction. *Educational Leadership*, *72*(6), 60–64.

Irizarry, J. (2015). What Latino students want from school. *Educational Leadership*, *72*(6), 66–71.

Kovarik, M. (2014). Tell ELL's about culture. *New Teacher Advocate*, *22*(1), 3.

Krashen, S. (2004). *The power of reading: Insights from the research*. (2nd ed.) Portsmouth, NH: Heinemann.

Olsen, L. (2010). *Reparable harm: Fulfilling the unkept promise of educational opportunity for California's long term English learners*. Long Beach, CA: Californians Together.

Planty, M., Hussar, W., Syder, T., Provasnik, S., Kena, G., Dinkes, R., & Kemp, J. (2008). *The condition of education 2008* (NCES 2008-031). Washington, DC: National Center for Education Statistics.

Segal, B. (2014). 4 reading strategies to give ELLs understanding and confidence. *New Teacher Advocate*, *22*(1), 18–19.

U.S. Department of Education. (2005). Developing programs for English Language Learners: Glossary. Retrieved from: http://www2.ed.gov/about/offices/list/ocr/ell/glossary.html

Zimmerman-Orozco, S. (2015). Border kids in the home of the brave. *Educational Leadership*, *72*(6), 48–53.

CHAPTER 5

Children's Literature and Cultural Experiences beyond the Classroom

My Life Graphic/Shutterstock.com

Much of this book has focused on bringing appreciation and understanding of cultural diversity to classrooms already populated by students of various races and ethnicities. As indicated in Chapter 1, diverse classrooms are a growing phenomenon in U.S. schools and teachers need to be prepared to create inclusive learning environ-

Juliya Shangarey/Shutterstock.com

ments that will lead to the academic success of all students. Nevertheless, it must be recognized that as recently as 2013 White-non-Hispanic individuals constitute over 60% of the US population (U.S. Census Bureau, 2015). Thus, it follows that many schools, and for that matter entire school districts, may have few, if any racial minority students. Moreover, many of these same schools and/or districts may have few if any ethnically diverse students who would otherwise fall into the White-non-Hispanic population category. The point being made here is that teaching diversity in non-diverse settings can present challenges that we have not yet addressed. Diverse classrooms bring together students from various races and ethnicities, along with their cultures and often languages other than English. Such classrooms, in and of themselves, are student-learning experiences in diversity; even without formal instruction. Students in nondiverse, predominantly White-non-Hispanic settings do not have the benefit of classroom interaction with other races and ethnicities. Yet, these students will eventually move on to other school settings and the world of work and will inevitably encounter greater diversity in terms of student and/or work colleagues. We must ensure that these students are prepared with the knowledge and appreciation of a wider range of races and ethnicities to facilitate their life transitions. Once again, children's literature can play a key role in this process, as unfamiliar cultures can be introduced in an enjoyable and positive manner through reading. However, especially in these nondiverse classrooms, let's consider bringing cultural contacts into the classroom to add even greater exposure to diverse ethnicities and races; although to be clear, such contacts and the activities that bring them about, are certainly appropriate for classrooms of any diversity composition.

Pen Pal Activities

Establishing pen pal relationships with students in other schools can be an excellent starting point for bringing different cultures into a classroom. Teachers should use their professional networking opportunities to explore mutual interests in establishing pen pal relationships for their classes. Also, opportunities to establish these kinds of relationships are often posted on websites such as the following:

iQoncept/Shutterstock.com

- *School Pen Pals and Keypals*

  http://www.theteacherscorner.net/penpals/

  Summary: The Teacher's Corner has made it effortless to find penpals for students. Just by clicking on a place on the globe, educators can arrange pen pals in an effort to broaden their students' horizons. Pen pals are arranged based on grade and even foreign countries like the Philippines and New Zealand participate.

- *Pen pal Schools: A World of Learning*

  https://penpalschools.com/

  Summary: A standards-aligned, 6-week pen pal program that pairs students all over the world. Students can practice their foreign language skills and learn more about other countries. This website also provides educators with cross-curricular assignments.

Teachers can make contact with classroom teachers in other schools to make appropriate arrangements for establishing these pen pal relationships. Selecting a particular school/classroom need not be based on criteria such as exotic location or distance between the two groups of students. Rather, consideration can be based on what the two groups of students can learn from and share with each other, such as their cultural backgrounds, nature of the communities in which they live, and activities they engage in, both in and out of school. Thus, an obvious pairing would be a rural, non-diverse classroom with an urban, diverse classroom.

Another mutually beneficial pairing might be a non-diverse class with one that is populated with many students whose primary or family language is not English. Perhaps venturing farther afield but still staying within the United States, seeking out pen pal relationships with Native American students, as well as students in Hawaii, Alaska,

Puerto Rico or the U.S. Virgin Islands, would create pairings that would be mutually beneficial to each group of students. And of course, if the opportunity exists, establishing pen pal relationships with students in another country would surely be exciting and a tremendous cultural learning experience.

Pen Pals in the 21st Century

Not too long ago, the meaning of the term pen pals was self-explanatory, that is, it involved two people writing letters to each other, using pens and paper, which would then be inserted into envelopes and mailed via the Postal Service. To be clear, there is nothing wrong with this age-old tradition and it can still be the process used for classroom pen pal relationships. In fact, many teachers might prefer this process for writing evaluation purposes (an important skill development by-product of a pen pal program). However, just as technology has reduced our reliance on "snail-mail" generally, we now have electronic alternatives to the traditional hard copy pen pal process, most notably email, online chats, video conferencing, *Facetime* and *Skype*. In fact, while the traditional hard copy pen pal process can be effective in establishing introductory relationships between students, emails and online chats can serve that same purpose as well as facilitate other learning activities beyond introductions. For larger group activities, video conferencing and *Skype* can also be used for communication between the two classes.

Bringing Children's Literature into the Virtual World

Returning to the focus of this book, using diverse children's literature in teaching diversity can take place in the virtual world between students or groups of students in two different classrooms. For example, each class can be assigned the same book to read and then it can be discussed between each pairing of students via email or chat or in groups such as literature circles using *Skype* or video conferencing. The selected books could feature a racial or ethnic group common to one of the classes. Under this scenario, one class would benefit from reading a book that portrays this culture of many of its class members while the other class would gain knowledge and perspective of this culture from both reading the book and discussing it with members of this culture. Another scenario can involve both classes

parinyabinsuk/Shutterstock.com

Gladskikh Tatiana/Shutterstock.com

reading a diverse book that features a culture that is not common to either group. One-on-one and/ or group discussions may surface different perspectives based on the different backgrounds of the two classes. In either scenario, children can also be asked to complete Venn Diagrams that can also be completed during student discussions to compare and contrast their respective experiences reading these books and how these are similar to or portray their own lives.

Gladskikh Tatiana/Shutterstock.com

Among books summarized elsewhere in this volume that could be read in conjunction with these activities include:

- *Number the Stars* by Lois Lowry,

- *Esperanza Rising* by Pam Muñoz Ryan

- *My Name is Sangoel* by Karen Lynn Williams

- *One Green Apple* by Eve Bunting

Other books that would complement pen pal discussion opportunities include the following:

- *Catch Me the Moon Daddy* by William Kaufman

  Summary: Selected photos and lullabies from different cultures and countries all over the world.

- *Child of the Civil Rights Movement* by Paula Young Shelton and Raul Colon

  Summary: An inside account into the culture of the Civil Rights movement of the 1960s and the terrible Jim Crow laws of the American South. This story is recollected by Paula Young Shelton, daughter of civil rights leader Andrew Young, and contemporary of Dr. Martin Luther King, Jr. Paula recounts stories about her and her family not being allowed into White-only restaurants, and her first "protest" by crying in a restaurant when they were not allowed to be seated because of the color of their skin. She remembers seeing news reports on television with her parents about the Freedom Riders and how they were attacked and their buses burned. This story inspired her parents to move to Georgia and join the movement with Dr. King. She was under the dinner table in her parent's house when all of the most notable civil rights leaders of the day planned the Selma, Alabama protest march. The reader experiences the difficulties of being a person with black skin in the segregated South.

- *First Year Letters* by Julie Danneberg

    Summary: First year teacher Mrs. Hartwell sets up a post office letterbox in her classroom. Through the children's letters to their teacher, the reader gets a glimpse into the hilarity and drama that can fill an elementary classroom. The letterbox is a means by which Mrs. Hartwell gets her students' writing, which in turn gives them plenty of practice; hence they see their penmanship improve also. The students learn how invaluable their teacher is to them, and the teacher learns from the students in return.

- *Me on the Map* by Joan Sweeney

    Summary: A young children's book that teaches readers about finding their place on a map. The narrator begins small with a map of her bedroom. It leads to a map of her street, then her town, and so on. The narrator also shows the reader how they can find their town on a country map, and also on a world map. The narrator makes the powerful statement that she is not the only child with a special place on a map of the world. There are other children just like her.

Other activities can then evolve from these virtual discussions. For example, book discussions can include interpretations of illustrations in the books they are reading. Students from each class can be asked to create their own book cover for their assigned books. Also, in instances where the book(s) being read involve a foreign land, students could be asked to compile a list of what they would bring to this country and why, if they were permitted only one suitcase. These answers could be compared using a summary chart to identify both similarities between the two classes, as well as differences that may be culturally driven.

Anastasiia Kucherenko/Shutterstock.com

As for more advanced activities, consider assigning culturally diverse biographies to pairs of students from each class. Then using email, chat, and/or Skype (or regular mail), each pair of students would then interview each other for the purpose of creating a biography (to date) of their partner. The interview can include culturally based questions under the guidance of the respective classroom teachers and appropriate (usually early life) elements of the biographies they read, can serve as models. The student-created biographies can be shared between partners as well as with both pen pal classes.

Among the book choices that can facilitate this activity are:

- *A Child's Alaska* by Claire Rudolf Murphy

    Summary: Packed full of facts about Alaska, Claire Rudolf Murphy tells a story of what it is like to live in a state so disconnected and unique from the rest. "Rural" is not enough to describe how remote

    parts of Alaska are. We know it is cold but *A Child's Alaska* educates readers on everything that makes up Alaskan culture.

- *Anna's Athabaskan Summer* by Arnold Griese

    Summary: In flowery language, Arnold Griese describes a "typical" day for an Athabaskan child. All members of the family are hard at work and readers learn different routines that keep things at home running smoothly. The story also dives deeper by revealing some cultural beliefs regarding hunting and the appreciation of nature. *Anna's Athabaskan Summer* is an interesting narrative full of valuable cultural information.

- *At Ellis Island: A History in Many Voices* by Louise Peacock

  Summary: The author mixes true vignettes from immigrants and the people who worked at Ellis Island alongside a fictional story written by the author. The book has a wonderful array of various and diverse cultures seen in the vignettes presented by the author. The story by the author may be fictional, but could embody any of the millions of immigrants that came to United States through Ellis Island.

- *Journey to Ellis Island* by Carol Bierman

  Summary: In *Journey to Ellis Island,* the reader is introduced to the Russian Jewish culture with the author's story about her father's quest to come to the United States in 1922. He came to the United States on a steamer ship as a third class passenger with his mother and sister. They escaped the ravages of war and faced discrimination at every turn. It was their determination for a better life in the United States that supported them in their dramatic journey.

thomas koch/Shutterstock.com

- *Listen to the Wind* by Greg Mortenson and Susan L. Roth

  Summary: A lost, injured hiker finds his way into a remote, mountainous Pakistani village. The villagers take him in and care for him. As he heals, he sees the local children are in desperate need of a schoolhouse. He promises to return to the village with the supplies and materials needed to help the villagers build their schoolhouse. Based on a true story.

- *The Dreamer* by Dr. Bobbie Solley

  Summary: Clarissa is a young girl from Haiti who finds she is missing the structure of a classroom and the learning environment when school lets out for the summer. As her siblings and other kids in the neighborhood play their summer games, Clarissa is bored. She sees her dolls and dreams of becoming a teacher. She practices being a teacher in front of her dolls, and over the course of the summer, her siblings and other neighborhood kids join her "classroom." Clarissa eventually attends college and sees her dream of becoming a teacher come to fruition as she returns to her hometown to teach. Based on a true story.

Another more advanced pen pal activity involves the use of Reader's Theater. Reader's Theater is reading-aloud in order to tell a story. It is an activity that helps improve reading comprehension, fluency, builds confidence, motivation, expression while reading, and provides a purpose for reading.

Scripts can be purchased, found online for free that are already written, or students can write scripts themselves. It does not require students to memorize scripts and involves little if any costumes or props; nor are background sets anticipated.

Reader's Theater as a virtual activity begins with each pen pal class being assigned to read culturally based traditional tales and then placed in groups (within each class) according to a particular tale they read. Each group would then prepare a script about the tale they read, that they would share with their own class as well as their pen pal class; using video conferencing or *Skype*. Once this process is complete, the groups from each class would exchange scripts and perform the tale using the other class group's script. Discussion can then follow on the differences in each presentation even though the same book or story was the basis for each script. The learning opportunity that can present itself in this activity is that the interpretation of the story reflected in each script can vary with cultural backgrounds of those who created it.

Among books that can be read to facilitate these Readers' Theater activities include:

- *The Jolly Postman or Other People's Letters* by Janet and Allan Ahlberg

  Summary: A delightful book about the postman who brings the mail to all the characters in various children's fairy tales. The pages each have actual letters that the jolly postman brings to each character.

- *The Sneetches* by Dr. Seuss

  Summary: *The Sneetches* is a story about diversity and acceptance. The Star-Belly Sneetches think of themselves as far more superior than the Plain-Belly Sneetches and turn up their noses at them. Plain-Belly Sneetches weren't included in any of the fun. One day, Sylvester McMonkey McBean comes to the beach with a contraption that would put stars on the Plain-Belly Sneetches—of course, they all lined up. The original Star-Bellies used the contraption to remove their stars so they could still differentiate themselves from the other group of Sneetches. After many rounds of this, it was time for Sylvester to pack up and go. By then, the Sneetches had lost track of who originally had stars and who didn't. The Sneetches decided to forget about the stars and lived together as one.

- *Why Mosquitos Buzz in People's Ears* by Verna Aardema

  Summary: One day a mosquito annoys an iguana by telling one of his ridiculous stories. The iguana puts sticks in his ears to ignore him and ends up ignoring his friend, the snake. This angers the snake who chases after the rabbit. This domino effect of animal conflict ends up upsetting the owl who refuses to let the sun rise. The King Lion traces all of it back to the mosquito and to this day, mosquitos buzz about their guilt in people's ears until *SPLAT*.

Again, a basic premise of these activities is to use children's literature as a segue to contacts between children from different racial and ethnic backgrounds, when one class is more diverse than the other. However, a particular advantage can be gained when both classes have common language ELL students. Pairing these students

together as pen pals can help to bridge their respective English language deficits; and if one of these students is in a non-ELL predominant classroom, that student's comfort level can be increased through this type of pen pal relationship, as well.

In any event, using children's literature as a basis for pen pal relationships clearly falls within Gay's (2000) definition of culturally responsive teaching: "using the cultural knowledge, prior experiences, frames of reference, and performance styles of ethnically diverse students to make learning encounters more relevant to and effective for them." (p. 29)

Establishing Pen Pals with Prospective Teachers

Thus far, we have considered ways to use children's literature as the basis for pen pal relationships among students attending different schools, with the pairing of non-diverse and diverse classrooms offering particularly good opportunities to expand cultural horizons. An alternative approach that has proved beneficial to lower income and/or predominantly minority classes and schools, has involved establishing pen pal relationships with prospective teachers in colleges and universities. Through contacts with local or even distant undergraduate college/university education departments, classroom teachers, and/or their school leadership may be able to arrange for prospective teachers to become pen pals with their students. Conversely, some universities have sought out these arrangements with school districts in order to broaden the cultural horizons of their prospective teachers and even to provide online tutoring assistance to students. In either case, this type of arrangement provides disadvantaged school students with an opportunity to interact with college students about their respective lives, activities, goals, and so on. Particularly for lower income, minority students, this type of interaction may provide personal insight to future educational and career opportunities to which they are not frequently exposed. For the college students, they too may become involved in interactions with children from backgrounds with whom they may have had little exposure and thus, this arrangement can be a culturally broadening experience for them, as well. For instance, one university initiated a pen pal program introduced largely to nondiverse college students/prospective teachers to elementary students attending a predominantly black urban school. Another university-initiated program collaborated with a rural Alaska school district that is largely populated with little-known Native Alaskan ethnicities. While this program started modestly using postal correspondence, it expanded to communicate via *Skype* and *Blackboard Collaborate* for purposes of tutoring; another to benefit to college students/prospective teachers as they are able to hone their instructional skills. See McMillon (2009) and Bazley (2010, 2015) in the Supplemental Resources section to read more about these kinds of programs.

Supplemental Resources for Teaching Diversity and Multiculturalism through Children's Literature
Articles

- Bazley, K. (2015). Focus on elementary: Expanding cultural awareness through online elementary tutoring. *Childhood Education, 91*(3), 212–214.

  Summary: Using *Blackboard Collaborate*, Kutztown University preservice teacher candidates are working with native Alaskans living in extremely rural, isolated villages. They gain experience working with students from unfamiliar cultures and polish their beginning teaching skills.

- Bazley, K. (2010). Looking northward at cultural awareness and preparing teachers. *Teacher Education, 12*(2).

  Summary: Beginning with a pen pal project, preservice teachers at Kutztown University had the opportunity to take this experience much further. The preservice teachers made standard-aligned lessons for children in Alaska and some even had the opportunity to travel to these rural Alaskan villages and put their teaching skills to the test. Not only did the preservice teachers gain advantageous teaching experience, the students in Alaska benefited from the individualized instruction and from the relationship they had with their pen pal. These students rarely have contact with people outside of their village, so it was a valuable learning experience for all.

- McMillon, G. T. M. (2009). Pen pals with borders: A cultural exchange of teaching and learning. *Education and Urban Society, 42,* 119–135.

  Summary: This article discusses how imperative it is that teacher education programs create effective ways to teach preservice teacher candidates to meet the needs of diverse students. The article examines a pen pal cultural project between preservice teachers and students in an urban elementary school.

- Montgomery, W. (2001). Creating culturally responsive, inclusive classrooms. *Teaching Exceptional Children, 33*(4), 4.

  Summary: Montgomery provides several instructional methods that fit the needs of diverse learners. From cross-curricular materials and ways to involve parents, this article is a comprehensive guide for educators of diverse students.

- Holloway, J. H. (2003). Managing culturally diverse classrooms. *Educational Leadership, 61*(1), 90–91. Retrieve from http://www.ascd.org/publications/educational-leadership/sept03/vol61/num01/-Managing-Culturally-Diverse-Classrooms.aspx

  Summary: This article offers insight on considerations to make when managing a culturally diverse classroom. Classroom management techniques are not universal. Holloway discusses best practices for classroom management with students of diverse backgrounds.

- Pagés, J. M. (n.d.) *Learning tip #47: Pen pals and keypals can motivate children to write.* Retrieve from http://www.kidbibs.com/learningtips/lt47.htm

Summary: This online article includes links to everything a teacher would need when setting up a pen pal program/unit. There are links to sites to arrange pen pals, letter writing resources, and a book list that features characters who write letters.

Websites

- *School Pen Pals and Keypals*

  http://www.theteacherscorner.net/penpals/.
  Summary: See Above

- *Managing a culturally Diverse classroom*

  http://www.glencoe.com/sec/teachingtoday/weeklytips.phtml/230
  Summary: Five steps, one for each day of the week, that teachers can do to create welcoming, successful, diverse classrooms.

- *Six Reasons your kids should have a pen pal*

  http://www.ouradventurestory.com/6-reasons-your-kids-should-have-a-pen-pal/
  Summary: Not only is having a pen pal fun, it's educational. Here are six reasons your kids should have a pen pal.

- *Teaching Tolerance: Culture in the Classroom*

  http://www.tolerance.org/supplement/culture-classroom
  Summary: Breaking cultures down based on heritage is easy but it's true that each person's cultural identity is truly unique. It's important for educators to be aware of their own biases and learn more about the culture of their students. This website speaks to this as well as creating connections among students.

P. Chinnapong/Shutterstock.com

References

Bazley, K. (2015) Focus on elementary: Expanding cultural awareness through online elementary tutoring. *Childhood Education, 91*(3), 212–214.

Bazley, K. (2010). Looking northward at cultural awareness and preparing teachers. *Teacher Education, 12*(2).

Gay, G. (2000). *Culturally responsive teaching: Theory research, and practice.* New York, NY: Teachers College Press.

McMillon, G. T. M. (2009). Pen pals with borders: A cultural exchange of teaching and learning. *Education and Urban Society, 42,* 119–135.

U.S. Census Bureau. (2015). *USA quick facts.* Retrieved from http://quickfacts.census.gov/qfd/states/00000.html